# The
# COUNTRYSIDE
# BOOK

BLOOMSBURY

LONDON · NEW DELHI · NEW YORK · SYDNEY

# The
# COUNTRYSIDE
# BOOK

Tessa Wardley

101 ways to relax, play, watch wildlife
and have adventures in the countryside.

BLOOMSBURY
LONDON · NEW DELHI · NEW YORK · SYDNEY

Bloomsbury Natural History

An imprint of Bloomsbury Publishing Plc

50 Bedford Square
London
WC1B 3DP
UK

1385 Broadway
New York
NY 10018
USA

www.bloomsbury.com
BLOOMSBURY and the Diana logo are trademarks
of Bloomsbury Publishing Plc

First published 2015
© Tessa Wardley, 2015
© 2015 illustrations and photographs by Tessa Wardley
© 2015 in other photographs remains with the individual photographers
– see credits on page 208.

British Library Cataloguing-in-Publication Data
A catalogue record for this book is available from the British Library.
ISBN (PB) 978-1-4081-8703-6
ISBN (epub) 978-1-4081-8705-0
ISBN (epdf) 978-1-4081-8704-3

10 9 8 7 6 5 4 3 2 1

Designed by Nicola Liddiard, Nimbus Design
Printed and bound in China

To find out more about our authors and books visit www.bloomsbury.com.
Here you will find extracts, author interviews, details of forthcoming events
and the option to sign up for our newsletters.

For my adventurous and gorgeous girls:
*Anousha*, *Thea*, *Poppy* and *Lottie*.

Mountain, moorland, weald and downland;
fenland, breckland, scrub and parkland.
Grassland, heathland, rock and hedgerow;
woodland, wetland, coast and meadow.
The country beside us is constant, unchanging;

everyday colour a backdrop of green.
But look a bit closer and the detail's exciting,
enticing, enchanting; adventure unseen.
The familiar and ordinary with more exploration
is strange, unexpected and vividly green.

**We should all have** our own little slice of countryside to call our own, to hold close to our hearts. A meadow, rock, tree; visit it often and make it special by knowing every sight, sound and sensation of every season, time of day and weather condition. Slip into your own little envelope of country a place to observe, without being observed, merge in.

If Norwich resembles the eye of Norfolk's Cyclops then my early country envelope would have been its nose and mouth. A happy, pizza-slice of land bounded by the main roads to Ipswich and Bungay with the River Waveney to the south, and the Yare to the north, this is agricultural land, undulating and richly mosaicked with fields, lush hedgerows and woods. My father's daily pilgrimage to work in Norwich later became my own and eventually I became blind to my surroundings.

Leaving home after my A levels I was anxious to see more of the world. I raised some funds and set off with a friend, working and travelling, experiencing life and revelling in the immensely

different surroundings that we encountered on the way.

We saw many places and had many wonderful experiences and memories to take with us. But one of my strongest memories comes from the first few days back home. I remember so clearly the feelings of wonder and joy at seeing my familiar patch of land. Having become used to experiencing new places I was looking so much more carefully at what was in front of me, I was seeing it all as if for the first time. I was stunned. We go off travelling around the world to vast, desiccated continents but we have such beauty and abundance all around us at home.

It was July and the countryside was fizzing with life. Road margins were bursting with growth: dense, luxuriant green, dotted with red poppies, blue cornflowers, yellow buttercups and dandelions. The fields were full to bursting and the hedgerows were impenetrable, positively humming with insect life. The sky was an improbable blue, punctuated with airy white clouds. My early morning journey into the city

was criss-crossed with Weasels and shrews and Rabbits, a Kestrel hovered over the road verge, while Swifts and Swallows swooped over the golden cornfields. As I passed along the river valley the early morning mist was still clinging mystically to the water meadows. Tense strands of cotton wool, the dense white of swans' plumage, were slowly pulling apart, creating negative space as if made from an accumulation of the mist. Nothing I had seen on my travels had beaten this journey: the sight was uplifting and I felt I was discovering something more about myself and my place in the world.

The natural world becomes alive to us as we begin to take notice of it. But if we live our lives engaging with nature then it is we who are now really living. Activities undertaken in green spaces have been shown to be so much more beneficial when compared to the same activities undertaken in the built environment. Being in the countryside takes us outside physically and emotionally – it brings people out of themselves and maybe that is where we are able find our true selves.

Before I went off on my travels and then saw my own countryside through the eyes of a tourist I had never really understood tourists who came to our country. Canadian and Australian relatives would come back time and again exclaiming about the beauty and the history, it was finally beginning to dawn on me what they had seen.

No one ever really appreciates what they have right outside their door; as Joni Mitchell said 'you don't know what you've got 'till it's gone'. Our televisions are full of the most amazing wildlife programmes, fantastic images of big game and endangered habitats but maybe, we should remember to get out and enjoy the wonder and beauty of our own surroundings. Or maybe it is only with a view of the wider world that we can really appreciate what we have.

Mountain, moorland, weald and downland: the British countryside comes in many forms and beyond our towns and cities it is our home. Our ancestors feared the natural world and did their best to tame it. They were so successful that now we fear for its ultimate survival. Our knee jerk reaction is to continue our regime of control and try to replace what we are in danger of losing. We have come so far from our early reliance on nature that we have forgotten how to coexist with nature. We are part of it: we must relax, stand back and give it space. Like our children, given encouragement and space it will find its own way, and maybe we don't need to control it.

But let's not make a burden of the countryside experience. Let's not go outside to have an 'experience' or some kind of 'communion' let's just get outside as much as we can, have some fun and see how good it makes us feel.

The best way that we can begin to appreciate what we have is to get out in it. Don't agonise over it today; enjoy it, live in it, play in it. The rest will follow.

Find your outside place; a place where you can find yourself.

# How to use the book

The introductory chapters of the book will explain a little about the countryside, and the variety of the habitats that you may experience as you travel Britain. If you need help finding a particular habitat type the section on 'Finding habitats' may help. The countryside is all around us and all we need is a little understanding to be able to enjoy it to the full. So, arm yourself with a map and you will be set to get out there and find your own slice of countryside.

Within the rest of the book are five sections full of activities to suit the way you feel, whether you want to relax, play, be curious, have an adventure or answer some questions.

Most of the activities start with a journal extract where I convey the images that captured my imagination. In most cases this is followed up with 'how to' sections that give more detailed information, which should enable you to try out or refine the activities that may or may not be familiar to you. Where relevant there are also notebook sections which provide all sorts of information about the countryside – the wildlife, geography, mythology, natural history or just stories that will enrich the experience.

The underlying philosophy of this book, if there is one, is one of simple fun. Strip out all the unnecessary clutter of life, just go out for the day and have fun with what you find. You don't need bags of specialist equipment. There is always something around in the countryside on which to build a game, investigation or adventure without the need for hours of planning and bags of kit.

Getting outdoors is a great way to challenge the ties of technology and get some fresh air, a bit of exercise, nourish your senses and be inspired. The fact that it is easy on the pocket and the environment is a bonus.

*The Countryside Book* will give you the confidence to side step the work hard, play hard, walk fast mentality; to indulge your inner child, and just go outside for the sake of getting outside. Revel in the freedom, feel a little wild and feed your curiosity. It is free, simple, environmentally friendly and therapeutic.

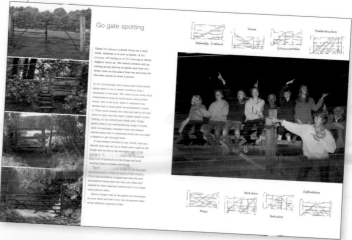

## Countryside habitats

The countryside is all around us and this book
deals with the range of habitats that you will
encounter: mountain, moorland, weald and
downland, fields and verges, heaths and
meadows The distribution of the different
habitats throughout the country is largely
controlled by the underlying geology.

### MOUNTAIN AND MOORLAND

Mountains and moorlands are the largest areas of
wild habitat in the UK. All are found in the
National Parks, particularly in England:
Dartmoor, Exmoor, the Peak District, Yorkshire
Dales, North York Moors, Northumberland and
Lake District; in Wales, Snowdonia and the
Brecon Beacons, and Scotland the Trossachs and

Cairngorms. Northern Ireland has no National
Parks but does have some rough mountainous and
moorland areas.

Although they seem wild and their physical
structure is beyond our control, even these
mountain habitats have been created by man.
Prior to human involvement they would originally
have been covered in scrub and woodland but a
long history of sheep grazing and in some areas
management by gamekeepers for grouse shooting
and deer tracking, has resulted in the heather
moorlands that predominate today. The only
really wild aspects are the rocky outcrops, wet
bog and some scree slopes that repel
management.

Typical vegetation is heathers and low moor
grass, bilberry and bracken with occasional
Rowan (mountain Ash) trees. Mammals are
typically deer, Fox and Mountain Hare and birds
include Buzzards, grouse, Golden Plover, Raven,
Skylark, Curlew and Meadow Pipit. Moths,
beetles, bees and spiders all enjoy the moorland
heather and rocks.

### WEALD AND DOWNLAND

The main area known as 'The Weald' is in
southeast England, an area of clay and sandstone
based lowland. Originally densely wooded and
still with extensive tree cover it is sandwiched
between two parallel chalk escarpments, forming
lines of hills known ironically as Downland – the
North and South Downs.

Other wealds and wolds exist in England, they
are typically open, rolling upland countryside and
include – the Yorkshire and Lincolnshire Wolds,
Cotswolds, North Weald in Essex and Harrow
Weald in London.

Chalk downland is an extremely diverse habitat for wildlife. The parallel chalk escarpments known as the North and South Downs reach from Kent through Wiltshire and on to Dorset, incorporating the isle of Wight. The distinctive White Cliffs of Dover on the south coast as well as the key features of Beachy Head, Seven Sisters, The Needles, Lulworth Cove and Old Harry Rocks are all part of the downland chalk beds.

The classic short-cropped grass of downland habitats is again a result of human intervention. The shallow soils of the chalk downs were too poor to support intensive agriculture so they were used for sheep grazing. These characteristically poor soils, along with the exposed conditions causing summer drought and winter frosts, have led to the unique assemblages of plants and animals that inhabit the grassland. The tough conditions mean that no single plant is able to take over and dominate allowing a wide variety of plants to struggle on. Typical plants may include cowslip, Kidney Vetch, Sheep's Fescue Grass and many species of orchid. As a result of the rich diversity of flowering plants, a rich insect life has developed, including several butterflies and moths found only on the downs. The blue Adonis and orange Gatekeeper are two such butterflies.

Downland habitat is at risk from development and road building, more 'efficient' farming practices and lack of grazing, allowing encroachment of scrub in some areas and over grazing in other areas.

## LOWLAND HEATH

Lowland heaths in the UK occur on acidic and impoverished peaty soils. Most of the extensive heathland habitat in the UK was created when man cleared woodland for livestock grazing but it still provides a sense of wilderness. Prior to man's involvement natural heathland would have been confined to small open areas grazed by deer and other wild herbivores. The area of heathland has decreased in recent years because of lack of management. If left it will revert to a more natural woodland scrub habitat, losing much of its typical heathland flora and fauna.

Heathlands are typified by the presence of small scrubby plants such as heathers and gorse as well as bilberry. Reptiles love heathland and snakes and lizards are commonly seen alongside specialist heathland birds such as the Nightjar, Stonechat and Dartford Warbler

The UK is very important internationally for heathland as 20 per cent of the world total heathland cover is found in the UK. Typical heathland habitats can be found in the New Forest in Hampshire, Brecklands of East Anglia, Ashdown Forest in East Sussex and other areas of Suffolk, Staffordshire, south and west England from Surrey to Cornwall, South and West Wales and the eastern Scottish Lowlands. There are some small areas in Northern Ireland mainly on the lower slopes of the Mourne Mountains and the Ring of Gullion

## FIELD MARGIN, VERGE AND HEDGEROW

The urban fringe, on the edges of fields, highways and railway tracks provide an enormous area of natural habitat in this country. These linear oases are extremely important for our native wildlife and provide corridors linking larger areas of open habitats. In the past road verges, railway lines and field margins were sprayed with herbicides and insecticides and cut back vigorously. These days they are much more likely to be left unsprayed and uncut and the quantity of life is astounding. Given our reliance on cars and trains in our daily lives these highway verges are probably the most viewed of all our national habitats. Verges reflect the local geology and the vegetation will vary from one area of the country to the next – look out for roadside heathers near moorland and heathland and flower rich hedges in the east and southwest.

Some road verges are still aggressively mown: if you see one that is over-managed get in touch

encourages a different flora than the grazing of it. Some plants can survive grazing but not mowing (Yarrow, buttercups and Picnic Thistle), while others can cope with mowing but not grazing (Meadowsweet, Sorrel Oxeye and Salad Burnet) (Rackham 1994).The timing of mowing and grazing will also affect the flora that are represented in a meadow.

### CHURCHYARDS

The church is a symbol of sanctuary for all who need it and in many areas it provides a wonderful refuge for wildlife. There is no one flora and fauna associated with churchyards. To an extent they reflect the countryside around but they also have their own characteristics, often supporting communities of exotic plants that have seeded from grave decorations. The ancient and undisturbed nature of many churchyard features encourages ancient assemblages, particularly of lichens on gravestones and trees especially the yew and its associated fauna. Reptiles and amphibians as well as bats tend to do very well in churchyards.

## How to find a nice bit of countryside

If your intention is to get out, wherever you are, to find a nice bit of countryside then there are several approaches to take. If you have a more focused desire to find a particular habitat to explore then you may need to undertake a bit more research before you set off.

Whichever approach you wish to take the best way to find a good spot in any give location is either to:

with your local council and ask them to follow Plantlife's guidelines for healthy verges see www.plantlife.org.uk.

### GRASSLAND MEADOWS

Grassland in this country is only maintained as grassland by grazing or cutting. Most grassland is really a grass crop, planted and cut for hay or silage and doesn't support the diversity of species that constitutes countryside grassland. Most meadows today exist only where they are common land and village greens or sometimes bordering rivers where they are too wet for planting. Some flower meadows have been saved from the plough by national and county trusts for conservation purposes. Cutting of meadows

**Talk to people** People who get out into the countryside regularly for work or pleasure will know the area well – dog walkers, horse riders, runners and mountain bikers usually cover a lot of ground in an area and can be a good source of information.

**Look at the local maps** On Ordnance Survey (OS) maps you should be able to spot paths, parking, nearby train stations and other activities that may be in the area. Open Access land is marked with a thick yellow band and indicates that you are free to roam on or off paths within the marked area – a great place to explore. Outside of Open Access land you must stay on paths.

**Search the internet** There are some really good websites that will help you find particularly nice places to get outside in your local area.

The Wildlife Trusts' national website www. wildlifetrusts.org.uk has a link to all local wildlife

trust websites. Your local Wildlife Trust website will have search engines for all local reserves which will allow you to chose the kind of setting you want for your day out.

The National Trust website, www.nationaltrust.org.uk, allows you to search for local National Trust sites which it lists with a description of the property or countryside it contains. All the websites let you search for sites in your area of interest and then link you through to a page for the sites that it identifies. Along with maps and directions you will find information on the wildlife you may expect to see and any facilities including, sculpture trails, cycle hire, cafes, parking and so on.

**Just go for a wander** Heading out in an area to explore on foot, bike, bus or car you will probably spot nice looking paths and open access land that you can then either investigate or research using the other tactics mentioned.

## Countryside access

The Countryside and Rights of Way Act 2000 (CRoW) ensured access to the countryside in England and Wales, which should mean that you have the right of access to all countryside. It is not quite as simple as that. On recent OS maps open access land is marked with a yellow boundary. Within this boundary line you are free to roam where you like at your own responsibility. You do not legally need to stay on the path – although it may be prudent to in some areas to avoid bogs and cliffs and other natural hazards. Outside of open access land boundaries the normal rights of way still exist.

### KEEP TO FOOTPATHS AND BRIDLEPATHS AND TRACKS

Woodland is not necessarily open access land. If there is a public right of way in to a wood you can walk through the wood but there is not necessarily legal access off the path, if there is not a foot or bridle path into the woods then there is quite probably no legal access allowed.

In simple terms in England and Wales you have legal access anywhere there is a footpath (these are clearly marked on OS maps as orange, green or a fine black dashed line). If the land is open access land you also have legal access off the footpath. Access land is marked on more recent OS maps with a yellow tint that replaces the purple outline on older maps.

Scotland has slightly different provisions as the Scottish Land Reform Act 2003 granted a 'right of responsible access' to land and inland water, which includes woodland. This continues the Scottish assumption that the public should have an unhindered access to the countryside and truly have the right to roam.

## A word on safety

Whenever you go out into the countryside remember that you are responsible for your own actions and those of your dependents. Take that responsibility seriously and remember that accidents can happen, especially important if you are off the beaten track. It is down to you to use your own judgement and as always when you are considering an activity and the abilities of your dependents if in doubt, don't. Use your common sense and wield your responsibility wisely but don't let it prevent you from having fun.

relax

# Watch the clouds

*North Downs, Surrey*

... We set off this morning in a fog so heavy it was almost a Victorian pea-souper. Beside the water meadows we passed through bands of fog of varying density, at times almost clearing, then shrouding us again in mystery. Rising up onto the North Downs, quite suddenly and unexpectedly, the clouds thinned, the sky above became a misty blue that quickly deepened and suddenly we were in the clear. The greens of the trees erupted, exuberant in their contrasting brightness and the sky became a deep, rich blue with sunlight slanting across it. As we reached a clearing at the edge of the downs, we found we were looking out over an undulating duvet of cloud. Thick and rich as whipped cream, it spread out as far as the eye could see. We had entered a magical land above the clouds, a place of fairy tales: Jack and the Beanstalk, Enid Blyton's *The Far Away Tree* and John Burningham's *Cloudland* all mixed into one. We almost felt we could see the children playing in the clouds and a castle sparkling in the distance ...

## How to watch clouds

It is hard to believe that these tangible 'ships of the sky' are made only from water vapour. The fog that sometimes envelops the landcape is simply clouds come down to earth. Every morning of my childhood holidays in the Lake District started with a walk down to the tourist information office before breakfast where they posted up the day's weather forecast including the cloud base – would today be a day for going up high or were we to be restricted to the valleys?

Being in the mountains allows you to get up close and personal with the clouds as they envelop you without warning, lifting and revealing exquisite views when you least expect it. Clouds create drama in the landscape as they allow the passage of shafts of sunlight, reminiscent of biblical scenes depicted in the early masters' oil paintings, and flow over ridges between valleys like waterfalls.

Being in the flat lands brings it own rewards. The big open skies give a 180° sky-view and provide superb cloud-watching opportunities. There is great entertainment in lying back on a bed of grass and watching the clouds scud by, changing shape as they go. The mix of fluid and solid provides ever-changing entertainment as the wind and the sun and the water play games in the sky. See if you can make out shapes and then watch them change. Take a camera and send some of your pictures in to the website of the Cloud Appreciation Society at: Cloudappreciationsociety.org.

The mix of fluid and solid provides
ever-changing entertainment as
the wind and the sun and the
water play games in the sky.

# Notebook · Clouds

A general knowledge of the different cloud shapes and what they foretell can be extremely useful in helping you to forecast the weather.

Clouds exist at three different heights as well as coming in different shapes. They are classified taxonomically, into genus and species like plants and animals, on the basis of their height and appearance.

At the most basic level of division the genera they can be divided into are:

## Cumulus clouds
These are the fluffy sheep we have all drawn as children. They are fair-weather clouds; they don't bring rain but accentuate a good day. Cumulus clouds can sometimes thicken and develop into rain clouds so it's worth keeping a weather eye open. A similar shaped cloud but one that sits higher in the sky is the **altocumulus**. They tend to be a layer of cloudlets, clumped together. At the highest altitude the similar shaped clouds are the **cirrocumulus**. They are even smaller cloudlets forming stippled sheets also known colloquially as mackerel skies. The cumulus group are the spiritual home of cloud watchers looking for shapes in the clouds.

## Stratus clouds
are low-lying sheets of thin, grey, misty, featureless cloud, the mother and father of drizzle. At a higher level they are **altostratus**, equally as featureless as stratus clouds but possibly slightly less oppressive and claustrophobic. At high level these thin sheets of cloud are known as **cirrostratus**, they can be so delicate as to be almost invisible on a sunny day until you put sunglasses on and the sun shining through them can form a halo effect.

Cirrus clouds are the very highest of clouds. These are the ones that look like streaks of hair and are often known as mares' tails. These innocent wafts of silk are harbingers of bad weather to come. They foretell of a change in the weather and often a developing front. The cycle may take up to two days but the **Cirrus** will thicken and spread across the sky to form cirrostratus, this then thickens and lowers to altostratus, accompanied by light rain. As this thickening and lowering continues **nimbostratus** develop. **Nimbostratus** are thicker and darker than stratus and bring the kind of heavy, persistent rain that can last all day. They are the home of cats and dogs. Once the nimbostratus is rained out over several hours the cloud changes to stratus breaking up eventually into **stratocumulus**. **Stratocumulus** is the transition when the depressing layer of stratus begins to break up and allow sunlight, texture and shape back in – but not quite the fluffy sheep of the cumulus that is next to follow.

Cumulonimbus are the last remaining genus – they are the towering, violent thunderclouds that reach from the lowest altitude right up to the very highest. They shed their rain in violent short outbursts of temper, exhausting themselves fairly rapidly.

# 26  Hare spotting

*Elmley Marsh, Isle of Sheppey, Kent*

... Our eyes searched the wide-open horizon, broken only by the occasional bird hide and raised slightly at the edges by the sea wall that closed off views to the estuary and sea beyond. Nearer, the sage-green of the marshes was broken by straw-like shafts of reeds, choking the waterways that criss-cross the marshes. In the falling light we could see an animal loping along towards us. Too big for a cat, a bit small for a dog, not quite the relaxed gait of a fox, it was camouflaged, merging into its background of marsh vegetation. It was spectacularly unconcerned by us and continued to come towards us apparently unaware, with the wind at its back, of our presence. All at once it registered our scent, sat back on its haunches and its shape was revealed: a Brown Hare. We looked at each other for a while before it jinked off into the undergrowth.

A couple of hours later we started our retreat along the mile or so track back to the road. Almost immediately we were caught by a Barn Owl: the most beautiful, silent, ghostly and ethereal of birds. It floated at eye height alongside the car, just a few metres from us, searching in the long grass for its next meal. As we travelled with it we slowly became aware of another body. In the grass below the owl, nibbling at the fresh young shoots, minding his own business, was our friend the hare. The hare just sat watching the world go by. The two were so entirely relaxed, continuing their business, untroubled by us that we stopped the engine and watched the show. It was live Attenborough magic without the commentary. We sat and watched as the owl searched and hovered above the hare, eyes piercing the thick swards of grass and bramble, occasionally stooping to flush out its prey and eventually making a killer dive. It captured a small creature and greedily ate it in one go, keeping its blank stare on its surroundings before flying off deeper into the marsh, away from the track and eventually out of sight. The hare, as if taking its cue, also ran off leaving us free to move on as well. The show was over ...

Too big for a cat, a bit small for a dog, not quite the relaxed gait of a fox, the hare was well camouflaged, merging easily into its background of marsh vegetation.

## How to find and watch hares

The Brown Hare (*Lepus europaeus*) that lives throughout England, Wales and lowland Scotland typically hangs out in open agricultural land and meadows; they also like marshland. They particularly enjoy fresh young shoots and so require a good supply of varied vegetation to eat throughout the year. Large fields of single crop plants don't suit them well, as once the plants have matured they are not soft and juicy enough for their liking. In recent years there has been a sharp decline in hare numbers in the west of the UK to the extent that they are almost extinct in the south west of England. This decline has been blamed on the move to silage production in dairy farming that relies on sowing single grass species for the silage harvest. You will have a much easier time trying to watch hares in the east of England where they fare much better in the arable areas.

Distinguishable from superficially similar Rabbits by their much longer legs, faces and black tipped ears, they also behave quite differently. While it is possible to confuse them when they are crouched down eating, as soon as

they start running or boxing they are immediately distinguishable.

Hares are usually nocturnal, solitary and shy creatures and can often be spotted in fields in the early morning through openings in hedges as you travel through agricultural areas. The exception to this rule is when they are mating. The female hare, known either as a doe or jill, only comes into season for a few hours at a time, so the male, the buck or jack, has to act fast. While in season and during daylight hours a single female is often pursued by a number of males. The unpredictable and crazy leaping and boxing behaviour that can

Brown Hare

Rabbits

often be seen is actually the female, in season, fighting off the males' advances. Only once the males have proven their strength and stamina will she succumb to mating. Although hares mate throughout the year there is a crescendo in spring that has led to their billing as 'Mad March Hares'.

So the best time and place to watch hares is in spring, in open agricultural land in the east of England, when they can sometimes be seen in large gangs behaving 'madly'. At other times of year an early morning trip to the fields and meadows may result in a solitary hare spotting.

# Notebook • The mythology of the hare

The characteristic behaviour of the hare has caused some fascinating mythology to build up around them both in Britain and around the world.

The hare's nocturnal nature has encouraged the perception of the animal as a moon gazer. Many works of art depicting hares also include a moon with the hare gazing at it or leaping around it. In Asia there has been observed, on the west side of the waxing moon – from the eighth day to the full – an image of a hare. In Sanskrit the word for the moon – sas nka – means 'having the marks of a hare'.

The hare is the fastest land mammal in the UK reaching speeds of up to 35mph. They are not only fast but very agile too, and this speed and manoeuvrability has led to further legends and myths. The ability to appear and disappear as they gallop and dodge at high speeds used to spook people into the belief that they had magical powers. In early Christian times hares were seen as shape-shifters and servants of the devil that could only be killed with a silver cross.

Possibly the most famous fable involving the hare is that of the hare and the tortoise. There are many variations on this story from cultures across the globe. Building on the theme of the hare as something of a fast moving wide boy they have also been attributed with the persona of a trickster. This has been incorporated into many traditional tales and stories with which you may be very familiar, for example the tales of Brer Rabbit.

Although hares are known for their running speed, their response to danger is actually to 'lie up'. They will crouch down very close to the ground in the hope that the danger will pass. This has made them very susceptible to some modern hazards such as pesticide sprays and also why they are typically the last animals to run from the corn as the harvester spirals towards the centre of the field. As the hare bolted at high speed from the last stand of corn the early farmers believed it to be Ceres, the Roman corn goddess, escaping in disguise. This also tied in with their reputation as a shape-shifter.

# Search for fairy rings

*Four Sticks, North Norfolk*

... My grandparents farmed in north Norfolk and my mother grew up there. The paddock at my grandparents' was always a good source of field mushrooms and Puffballs. When we went out to see Pixie, my mum's old pony, early in the morning, we would harvest them and have them fried in butter, on toast, for our breakfast. When riding Pixie we could see from the extra height that the mushrooms grew in rings on the grass and how, even when there were no mushrooms, darker rings of grass were still visible. I was told they were 'fairy rings' and if you stood inside them magical things would happen. I always wondered what those magical things would be but was always too terrified to try, so instead I would wend my way across the field, picking carefully around the outside of the darker green circles in case something awful should happen. In Rudyard Kipling's *Puck of Pook's Hill* the children perform a play in a fairy ring that causes Puck the fairy to appear. He then takes them on adventures with historical characters and, while I loved the story, it just convinced me further that avoiding the circles was the right thing to do ...

## What are fairy rings?

Fairy rings may be visible as a circle of darker green grass up to 10m in diameter. They are usually visible on the mown grass of parks and lawns or the rabbit-cropped short grass of chalk downlands or fields grazed by horses. In autumn and following rainfall the fungi that form these circles send mushrooms up above the ground where they can be clearly seen.

Two contrasting processes cause the colour change in the grass around the ring. Some fungi release growth hormones that actually encourage the growth of the lush green grass. In other rings, it is simply the contrast between the nutrient-depleted soil at the centre of the ring, caused by the growth of the mushrooms, with the healthier outer grass that shows the circle. The circle develops and grows as each generation of mushrooms depletes the soil in which they grow. When they shed their spores for the next generation of growth, only those that land outside the ring have sufficiently rich soil in which to grow. This causes the ring to grow year on year. Eventually the soil at the centre of the ring will replenish and you can sometimes see concentric rings as well as incomplete arcs and crossing arcs, as well as multiple circles in one area.

While these circles can be seen at ground level, any kind of elevation will provide a fantastic viewing of the patters – this may be achieved on a convenient slope above the ring, by climbing a handy tree or even on horseback!

Usually seen as just a
dark circle in grass, in
autumn and after
rainfall, the fungi that
form fairy rings send
mushrooms above the
ground where they
are easily seen

Savour the seasons

*1980s Norfolk*

... In intensively farmed Norfolk the signs of the seasons are dominated by the agricultural year. Our early jobs as teenagers were not shop work and waitressing but casual work helping out on the farms. Extra hands were always needed, particularly in the summer holidays, picking strawberries, thinning apples, weeding asparagus and bunching asparagus. I had one job bunching asparagus, where we were bussed from Norwich out to the fields. There was good camaraderie and banter amongst the labourers as worked our way along a row, side by side cutting the asparagus as we went. We had to collect stalks in a bunch, trim the ends nice and even, put an elastic band near the top and another an inch or so up from the bottom of the stalk before each bunch was packed into a crate. A supervisor wandered the field, checking that the bunches met his standards and every so often he would reject one or two. One day the poor guy working next to me had almost every bunch rejected. His were super skinny or bulging, with elastic bands missing or in the wrong places, ends all higgledy-piggledy. He just could not get the hang of it. Eventually he was told not to come back. I never worked out if that was his aim or if he really was that inept ...

## Seasons in the countryside

Even when we were not helping out with the farming year it was always important to know what was going on in the fields: ploughing, tilling, planting, harvesting – all had an impact on our daily lives. I remember many walks where we'd end up with feet triple their original size, weighed down by the recently ploughed clods of earth. Or at the other end of the season, pushing my way through fields of shoulder high rape in full flower – covered from head to toe in yellow pollen, sneezing away.

Aside from the jobs in the summer we would search out the field irrigators and run through the sprays and after the harvest climb on the bales of straw. There were agricultural shows to visit throughout the summer as well, with all the livestock and machinery to investigate. I always associate field poppies with the main show of the year – the Royal Norfolk Show – as the fields and hedgerows on the route to the show ground were always bursting with poppies during that first week of July – we would even get the day off school to go.

The end of the harvest was marked in my early childhood by the burning of the stubble. There was much excitement as my grandfather set fire to the dried stems of straw spiking sharply out of the soil. I was too young to help with beating out

It was always important to know
what was going on in the fields:
ploughing, tilling, planting,
harvesting – all had an impact on
our daily lives in the countryside.

the fire at the edges of the field to keep it in check, so we stayed back by the house watching progress. We were entranced by the excitement of the heat in the air, the haze over the field, the orange crackle and the pall of smoke that hung over everything. This is one ritual we never see now as it was banned in the 1990s mainly due to air pollution from the smoke.

Although these days I am only an onlooker in the agricultural seasons I still enjoy watching the changing seasons as the fields turn from brown to green to gold and back to brown again: the stripes and machinery, with attendant flocks of birds, and the swiss-roll bales of the harvested grass and corn. They all serve to remind us of what is going on around us as the world goes on turning.

For most of us the cycle of the seasons have less immediate impact on our daily lives but the turning of the earth and our circling of the sun are still integral elements of our year which resonate throughout all our activities. Just today I opened the back door and was immediately struck by the devil screaming of the swifts circling overhead – the indisputable evidence that summer is here; the world is still working.

We really are lucky in this country to have such tangible seasons, there is so much to enjoy throughout the year and each season we can welcome back our personal favourites. Some of the things I always look out for are:

## The best of spring •• It's green again, a vibrant lime green, with delicate leaves emerging all around and smells so alive.

- Bursts of colour; crocuses in parks and gardens, snowdrops, primroses and daffodils.
- Buds and catkins, wild cherry and crab apple blossom.
- Ferns unfolding in damp and shady corners.
- Cow parsley that springs up almost overnight, shoulder high on roadside and hedgerow.
- Massed bluebells and garlic in woods, a haze of colour between the trunks.
- Meadow flowers with butterflies flitting and bumblebees bumbling.
- At the water's edge: frogspawn, delicate damselflies, mayflies and swallows, House Martins and swifts.
- Mad March hares, the first cuckoo of spring, ladybirds emerging from hibernation.
- Cuckoo spit: a spot on every stem.
- The deafening dawn chorus.
- The promise of blackthorn and hawthorn in luxuriant candyfloss bloom.

## The best of summer •• Elderflower
plates mark the start of summer.

• Thick, lush, green, a blowsy blur, without sharp edges or definition.

• Fragrant honeysuckle, humming with insects.

• Cropped grass dotted with daisies and dandelions.

• Camp fires and sleeping out.

• Shooting stars.

• Foxglove spires collapsing in the hedgerows.

• Young ruffled birds taking their first shaky flights.

• Colourful crops: rape, linseed, golden corn, dotted with poppies.

• Discarded feathers as the birds moult.

• Insects hum, crickets and grasshoppers chirp, butterflies flit.

• Cut grass and summer smells, long endless days. Never getting to bed in good time.

## The best of autumn •• Purple-
plated orbs of elder berries announce the end of summer.

• Leaves turning brown, yellow and red burn in the dying sun.

• Harvest time: conkers, blackberries, sweet chestnuts, rowanberries, sloe berries, mushrooms.

• Earthy smells: fungus popping up everywhere.

• Sparkling spiders webs on a dewy morning.

• Migrating birds: swifts leave, swallows line telephone wires preparing for off.

• Fields turn brown as the stubble is ploughed in.

• Hunkering down, moving inside, nights close in, cosy wood fires...

## The best of winter •• A quieter time.

- Black and white colour schemes.
- Murmerations of starlings.
- Tree skeletons as the architecture of the countryside is revealed.
- Mosses and lichens show off their colours and shapes.
- The holly and the ivy.
- Winter wonderland magic with the promise of hoar frosts and early morning mists.
- Mistletoe balls.
- Seed heads in hedgerows: old man's beard and hogweed attract birds.
- Blackbirds and robins.
- Early nights for star watching and night walks.

# Watch the sunset

*Mewslade Bay, Gower Peninsular, Wales*

... At the end of the day we walked out onto the headland and, leaning back against the rocky slope watched as the sun slipped from sight. The banks of cloud alternately blocked and revealed the sun as it slowly fell towards the horizon, the colours shifting and changing before our eyes. Shafts of sunlight escaping from between the cloud would light up sections of the sea and islands before us, picking out highlights to focus on. As the last band of cloud was left above it the underside of the clouds were flooded in vivid colour: violets, purples and deep reds boiled and churned adding to the stripes of orange already burning like streams of molten rock across the horizon. The whole sunset merged and flowed as the colours slowly transformed. The sun dropped and, within minutes, the whole scene had changed as the sun finally slunk away, just leaving the memory of its final display in a gentle glow ...

## How to enjoy the sunset

The sun sets every day of our lives. It is entirely predictable and yet how many times will you really sit and enjoy it in your lifetime or take the time to make a feature of the sunset, sit down and really savour its full glory?

So often we will be rushing home from work, or school or rushing elsewhere when its glory is thrust into our consciousness. For once why not let the sunset take centre stage – plan for it and go and enjoy it.

If you are out in the countryside or can get there, the sunset is at its best under a big sky, without the interruptions of buildings. Not every day will have the full light show of colours and drama but keep your eyes open for an opportunity when the signs are good. A day of fine weather with some interesting looking clouds out to the west all bode well for a pleasurable sunset, so why not plan a little sunset expedition.

Think about somewhere you can go with a good horizon over to the western sky, may be up on a hill or a beach if you are really lucky, even across a field or a park can be great. You want to be able to see the sun get as close to the horizon as possible to see the best colours develop.

To be able to predict exactly where the sun will set and how long you have until sunset have a look at Sun magic on page 102.

Take some warm clothes – as even on a warm day the temperature drops quickly when the sun goes down. Go alone or take a friend, lover, children or dog. A blanket to sit on and some refreshment appropriate to your companions and mood. A notebook and camera to record the moment and a drink to toast a beautiful end to the day.

Once in place you can settle back and enjoy the show.

The sunset is at its best under a big sky, without the interruption of buildings ... a day of good weather with clouds to the west

# Star gazing

*August 12th, Can Sora, Pyrenees*

... Sitting on the balcony, wrapped in the warm caramel blanket of a humid summer's night, glass of wine in hand, head tipped back against the chair, the sky is alive with a myriad of silver pinpricks on a silvery shimmering sea. Every few seconds the scattering of light is shot through by a meteor and before we can fully register it another one elsewhere in the sky shoots off so that our eyes are continually on catch-up, never quite able to focus on any of the moving lights. The display continues for hours and we cannot drag ourselves away for fear of missing some of its magic. Transfixed we stay watching, necks cricking, wine glasses completely forgotten ...

## How to get the most out of the night sky

There are certain times of the year when meteor showers such as these occur frequently and, completely unplanned, we had happened upon one on a perfectly clear night in an area with virtually no light pollution. With a little planning and some luck with the weather you can maximise your chances of seeing a spectacular display.

### HOW TO WATCH STARS

The best place to watch the stars is as far away from artificial lighting as possible. This includes lights from cars and buildings as well as street lighting. The bigger the sky scape the better, so the big sky of the countryside is great for star gazing. Just don't go anywhere too wooded or into a deep valley.

Wherever you are in the UK you can usually see some stars on a clear dark night but certain parts of the UK have been given 'dark sky' designations which should mean they are saved from major light pollution. In a dark sky area it is possible to see the silvery backdrop of the Milky Way as well as the brighter stars of the major constellations.

Artificial lights are not the only source of light that can interfere with stargazing. The moon provides a large amount of ambient light and the full moon is so bright it can create a moon-shadow. Try to choose a dark night with no moon, but also a clear night with no clouds. The new moon comes around one night every month and if you get a cloud free night coinciding with the new moon then that is ideal. The days either side of the new moon when the moon is in its final stages of waxing and waning are also very dark and extend your stargazing opportunities. If it is summer time you may have to wait until after 11pm to get really dark conditions.

Your eyes can take 20 minutes to adjust fully to low light conditions so it will be a while before you can see all of the fainter stars. Try not to use a torch, or phones or apps too much to help you to acclimatise.

Certain parts of the UK have
been given 'dark sky'
designations which should mean
they are saved from major light
pollution and you will be able to
see stars far more clearly.

Make sure you have somewhere comfortable to watch from: a chair to sit on or a blanket to lie on will make your spotting more comfortable as will warm clothing. If you want to have some idea of what you are looking at take reference material: star maps, a book or stargazing websites and apps are great and some helpful ones are listed on page 45.

## DARK SKY DESIGNATIONS IN THE UK

The website www.darkskydiscovery.org.uk identifies places throughout the UK that have been designated as star gazing places. Some are darker than others and are designated as 'Milky Way sites' where you should be able to see the Milky Way with the naked eye. Less dark sites but still shaded from the worst light pollution are designated as 'Orion sites' and here it should be possible to see the seven main stars of the Orion constellation and therefore the main stars of all the Zodiac constellations. Internationally recognised dark sky locations are also identified and include such places as Exmoor, the Brecon Beacons in Wales, Northumberland, Galloway and the Isle of Coll in Scotland. Don't worry if you are not near one of these internationally recognised sites, wherever you live you should be able to find somewhere dark enough within half an hour that will enable you to look out for the major constellations and planets.

## DATES FOR METEOR SHOWERS

If you would like to see a good display of shooting stars there are certain dates in the Northern Hemisphere when meteor showers occur each year. If you can find somewhere dark on a clear night to watch the sky on any of these dates then you are guaranteed a great show.

| PEAK DATE | SHOWER NAME | FROM THE CONSTELLATION | METEORS PER HOUR |
|---|---|---|---|
| Jan 3/4 | Quadrantids | Left of Mizar/Alcor | up to 100 |
| April 21 | Lyrids | Lyra | up to 15 |
| May 5 | Eta Aquarids | Aquarius | up to 35 |
| July 29 | Delta Aquarids | Aquarius | up to 25 |
| Aug 12 | Perseids | Perseus | up to 80 |
| Oct 21 | Orionids | Orion | up to 30 |
| Nov 17 | Leonids | Leo | variable |
| Dec 13 | Geminids | Gemini | up to 100 |

**Source:** *The Night Sky*, Usborne Spotter's Guide series

## WEBSITES AND BOOKS FOR STARGAZING

If you are interested in gathering some more information about stargazing or want to have a more informed experience then there are some great observatories and star gazing events that will help you identify what you are seeing. Have a look at www.darkskydiscovery.org.uk to find out about activities close to where you live.

Philip's produce a planisphere which is a kind of star map that shows the position of the stars and constellations for every night of the year. You can get them for various positions across the globe. The one I have is for latitude 51.5°N, which is the right one to get if you are in the British Isles, Northern Europe, the Northern USA and Canada.

There are some great apps available for smartphones and tablets, some of them free, these allow you to hold your device up to the sky and it will show the position of the stars and constellations and their names.

If you want to investigate further on the Internet there are many sites that can lead you further into astronomy. Try the www.bbc.co.uk/science/space site or the www.skymaps.com sites to find out a bit more about what may be up there.

# Notebook · Key stars and constellations in the night sky

On a clear night you may be able to see as many as 3000 stars. To make sense of all those dots of light, astronomers group the stars into constellations. These constellations have been named after Greek gods and goddesses as well as famous heroes. Many Greek myths are stories that explain the formation of the constellations. Astronomy is the study of stars, planets and other bodies in the sky while astrology looks at the influence those bodies and their relative positions may have on our lives. Many cultures around the world have relied heavily on the portent of the stars in making major decisions, including when to marry and even when to go to war.

The earliest comprehensive records of the study of astrology come from Babylonian times some 1000 years BC when they divided the sky into the 12 zones of the Zodiac. Because it was hard to identify the boundaries of the zones in the sky the Babylonians attributed the names of the zodiac to particular groups or constellations of stars. Under the Greeks, and Ptolemy in particular (around 100 AD), the work of the Babylonians was formalised and recorded and set down in a form that is very little changed from the way that it is used today. Meanwhile in India, Hindu scholars independently developed a slightly different form of astrology.

## Some key constellations and planets to spot

***Ursa minor* (Little Bear)** This constellation is very important to those in the Northern Hemisphere as the star at the tip of its tail is Polaris, the pole star. This star sits over the North Pole and is therefore almost stationary and consequently a very useful reference point for navigation.

***Ursa Major* (Great Bear)** The brightest stars of this constellation make the Plough, a distinctive constellation in the northern sky, which is important because its two end stars point to Polaris, enabling its identification and use for navigation.

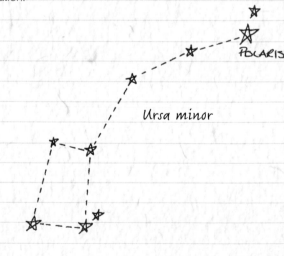

Ursa minor

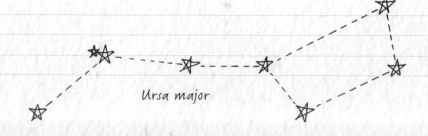

Ursa major

**Crux (Southern cross)** Easily Identifiable when in the Southern Hemisphere, the Southern Cross consists of four bright stars forming a cross, the central bar of which points to the South Pole.

**Orion (The hunter)** Orion is one of the most distinctive and easy to spot constellations as it contains several very bright stars, in particular: red Betelgeuse on one shoulder, the three stars of the belt and Rigel diagonally opposite Betelgeuse on the bottom corner of his tunic. Orion is particularly interesting because while Polaris, celestially speaking, sits over the North Pole, Orion sits over the celestial equator. This means its trajectory is always over the equator so we will always see it on our southern horizon as it moves from east to west every night. Because Orion is easily identifiable and over the equator he is always visible wherever you are in the world, although in the southern hemisphere it will be visible on the northern horizon and doing a handstand. The northern constellations of Polaris and the bears, will not be visible in the southern hemisphere and the southern constellations such as the southern cross are not visible to us in the northern hemisphere.

POLARIS

Canis major

**Canis major (Large Dog)** Canis major contains Sirius, the dog star, the brightest star of the sky. In Greek mythology Sirius is one of Orion's two dogs. The line of the three stars in Orion's belt points down to Sirius.

**Cassiopeia** An easily indentifiable 'W' shape and quite easy to spot, Cassiopeia was originally used to identify the extent of the Arctic Crcle. Polaris marked the North Pole, and the trajectory of Casssiopeia and Ursa major, circling around Polaris, described the outer edges of the Arctic Circle. It is now identified geographically rather than astronomically.

Count magpies

*Campervan, Norfolk to Exmoor*

... Every Easter my family and I made the long journey from Norfolk down to Exmoor to stay at my great aunt's hotel. Starting at the crack of dawn the six of us, two dogs and all our paraphernalia would pile into our orange VW campervan. In the days before compulsory seatbelts, we flattened all the seats into one big platform where we played all kinds of games on the journey: car cricket, twenty questions, spotting games as well as singing songs.

As we got closer we started to take more interest in our surroundings: rolling green hills dotted with yellow buttercups and white sheep, their young lambs leaping around and spiralling their tails. We would also see magpies. In Norfolk at that time magpies were quite unusual but in the southwest they were far more common. We would start saluting them for good luck and counting groups to work out whether we would be subjected to joy, sorrow, girls, boys, silver, gold or secrets never to be told ...

## How magpies can tell your fortune

If you see a single magpie when you are out and about it is always wise to give him a salute as you pass by ... The correct greeting is as follows: 'Good morning Mr Magpie, how is your wife this morning?'

If you greet a single magpie in this way you should ward off any bad luck that may be following the bird around. The reason this myth came about was that magpies usually mate for life. A single magpie suggests some misfortune has befallen its spouse. By asking the magpie how his wife is you are suggesting that he does in fact still have a partner but that she is just not there at that moment and all is well. So while a single magpie implies misfortune and sorrow, a pair of magpies suggests that all is well and that is the basis of the magpie fortune telling rhyme: 'One for sorrow, Two for joy'.

If you want to tell your fortune using the birds, the counting rhyme on the opposite page will give you some idea of what you can expect. Ten is the typical ending point for the rhyme but increasingly larger groups of magpies may be spotted at any one time. There is one version for numbers up to ten that continues:

*Eight for heaven,*
*Nine for hell,*
*Ten for the very devil himsel'*

There is no official contingency for numbers greater than ten but you can make up your own.

One for sorrow,
Two for joy,
Three for a girl,
Four for a boy,
Five for silver,
Six for gold,
Seven for a secret never to be told.

# Notebook · Magpies

Magpies are one of the easiest birds to identify; their striking black and white colouring, relatively large size and confidence in the urban environment and around roads make them very distinctive and easily visible. Their raucous, chattering conversation and upfront attitude have made them few friends, but when seen up close their plumage has an iridescent, petrol sheen and can be extremely beautiful.

As well as being the only animal that invites us to salute it, they are known for their interest in shiny objects that they will often take away to their nests. People who are attracted to and hoard interesting bits and pieces are often referred to as being a bit of a 'magpie'. Studies at the University of Colorado established that they are one of the few animal species able to recognise themselves in a mirror test and in spite of their apparently brash personalities have been known to mourn for their dead and even hold funerals for dead friends, gathering in groups and lying offerings of grass alongside the dead body.

There has been a significant increase in numbers of magpies in recent years. The RSPB believes their numbers have tripled in the last 30 years. There are a number of reasons for this. Until the start of the First World War, magpies were heavily persecuted by gamekeepers, bringing their numbers to a low

point. Since the Second World War they have not been under such pressure and their numbers have steadily increased. Magpies have been able to make the most of their lack of persecution and recover populations so rapidly because they are highly intelligent and adaptable birds. They are happy to nest near people so their urban and suburban populations have grown. Magpies will feed on a wide range of food sources, feeding from bird tables as well as taking young birds and mammals and feeding on road kill; they have benefited greatly from the increase in road traffic since the mid-20th century.

In recent years magpie populations have reached such levels that they are being blamed for the decline in songbirds. The culling of magpies has been suggested, but has not been agreed on a wide scale as there is no proven link between the magpie's increasing numbers and the songbird decline.

# Go gate spotting

Gates are always a great focus on a long walk, whether it is just to break up the journey, for racing to or for waiting at while laggers catch up. We nearly always end up taking group photos at gates and they are often used as the place that we will stop for the next snack or even a picnic.

In our increasingly well-manicured countryside, gates seem to be in better condition than I remember in the past. We came across many with complicated tying up techniques using binder-twine, bits of old wire, belts or whatever the farmer had to hand when he attempted to mend it. There were always the ones you had to lift and carry to open and the ones it really wasn't worth risking, so you would just climb over. Today, gates come in an overwhelming range of styles with increasingly complex close and release mechanisms that it sometimes feels like you need a degree to get through them.

It was always instilled in me, firmly, that you should only ever sit on or climb over a gate at the hinge-end as this is the strongest part of the structure. Climbing over away from the hinge puts a lot of pressure on the hinge and post, causing them to loosen and break.

Traditionally, different styles of five-bar gate predominated in different parts of the country. This regionalisation of gates has very blurred boundaries these days but they are often still named for their regional homes even if no longer restricted to them.

Have a longer look at the gates you encounter on your walk and see if you can recognise some of the different regional styles.

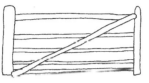
Dalmally, Scotland

Devon
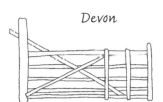

Gloucestershire

Pembrokeshire

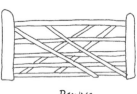
Powys

Yorkshire

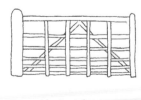
Yorkshire

Oxfordshire
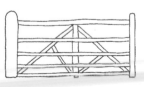

*Easter, Norfolk*

... We've just spent a beautiful day hunting for eggs in Norfolk churches. Misunderstanding the instructions we began by hunting high and low in Hempnall churchyard for a golden egg. We didn't know what size it was or where it was hidden and the churchyard is quite large. Luckily before too long we checked the instructions in the newsletter and discovered that the eggs were actually hidden inside the churches. There are eight churches in the group and we visited all of them in a single day. It was a perfect spring day, long grass and dandelions, cow parsley blowing and reflecting the scudding clouds in the sky. The churchyards were vibrant and alive with the buzzing of bees and the fluttering of butterflies. Once the egg was found we couldn't resist a quick search around the graveyards looking at the ancient and more recent gravestones and enjoying the abundance of life in this traditional place of death ...

## How to make the most of churchyards

Churchyards and graveyards are amazing places for natural history. Relatively undisturbed for thousands of years they are often real havens of wildlife. Ancient trees, particularly yews, abundant grasses and wildflowers are typical. Churchyards provide a sanctuary to the local wildlife of an area but more than that they often contain some exotic plants that have escaped from grave decorations and also attract some unique insects and birds.

Churches are a great way to get to know the history of a place. Many are left open to the public and if not, the churchyards nearly always are. Some churches have towers that are open to the public so you can get up high and see the surrounding countryside. This can be particularly interesting in flat areas where it is hard to gain any elevation. Ranworth Church is one of the few places in Norfolk where you can get a good view over the surrounding countryside.

The churches of an area give a real impression of the local history as they reflect the affluence and influences of the past. I recently discovered in Simon Jenkins' *England's Thousand Best Churches* that now-afffluent Surrey has just 13 churches of the on his list. This is because in the middle ages it was densely wooded, inaccessible and not particularly wealthy. Other counties, like Gloucestershire and Norfolk, became rich in the church building eras when agriculture and trading were so important and have 39 and 69 churches respectively in the top 1000.

The church was once the centre of every community. Whether you are a believer or not, a local church and its land have been in situ for many years and marked the comings and goings of the community. Stop in to the church and churchyard and see what it can tell you about the area you live in or are visiting.

Churches are a great way to get to know the history of a place. Many are still left open to the public and if not, their churchyards nearly always are.

play

*Lake District, October*

... It was the last day of our holiday in the Lakes so we went for a walk from Skelwith Bridge over to Elterwater and back. We stopped in the woods for a game of 'thicket' and to have a picnic. Lottie made squealing noises by blowing across a piece of grass stretched between her thumbs. Before long Hannah and Jacob joined in and, delighted by their success, continued as we walked on. As we emerged from the trees with the children still squealing we came face to face with a very impressive ram sporting rather fantastic 'pain au raisin' horns – and realised we had a triplet of buzzards circling overhead. They had been attracted by the apparent squeals of an injured rabbit and came to investigate. Presumably disappointed by the sight of three over-large prey, they drifted off adding their own mewing cry to the squealing grass ...

## Grass games

There are many games you can play with the humble grass and other path-side vegetation.

### SQUEALING
Pick a strong, green blade of grass and trap it between the sides of your thumb pads and the heels of your hand. Blow across the side of the grass where it is stretched across the gap formed when your thumbs are side by side. The resulting squeal sounds like a rabbit in distress and can attract or scare off predators and prey.

### GRASS RHYMES
One of our favourite grass games is the rhyme:

*Tree in summer,*
*tree in winter,*
*bunch of flowers,*
*April showers.*

This is performed with any grass seed head that you can run your fingers along to produce a 'bunch of flowers'. The fescue grasses (Fescues spp), bents (Agrostis spp) and Yorkshire Fog (Holcus lanatus) all have good 'tree' structures and work well for this game. The first line is the full grass. The second line the grass with seeds removed. The third line the bunch of seeds left in your pinched fingers and the final line the seeds thrown over your friend's head. Your friend will love picking seeds out of their hair for the next week.

### POP GUNS
I'll admit, the plantain is not a grass but it is a lot of fun and found growing on grassy verges.

This game was one of our family favourites when I was growing up. Using the plantain seed heads often seen alongside paths it would occupy us on long walks. Part of the trick is picking the right plantain for the job. It needs to be long enough to bend over as well as flexible enough to

The fescue grasses and Yorkshire Fog have good 'tree' structures with substantial seedheads that work well for the grass rhymes game.

bend – some can be brittle and just break. It also needs to be strong enough, once bent, to be able to pop the seed head off its stem. The right plantain can produce a very satisfying pop of several metres.

### GOOSE GRASS OR STICKY GRASS

Again, not grass but at least its common name calls it a grass. Goose grass is great fun for the person throwing but quite annoying for everyone else. This is another firm favourite on long walks. Goose grass is very sticky and clings satisfyingly to clothing. The best challenge is to sneak up on someone and stick a clump to their back without their noticing and see how far they go before they became aware.

### BURRS

The bane of a dog owner's life, burrs are variously sized balls of seeds that have little hooks on them and become attached to clothing and particularly tangled in dogs' hair. The Burdock produces barbed balls about the size of a cherry and apparently inspired the invention of velcro. Agrimony burrs resemble the heads of hedgehogs and look very cute until you get covered in them. Sticky grass/goose grass, as if it wasn't annoying enough, has miniature pea sized burs that really get in a good tangle, they start to appear in mid-summer and seem to go on forever. Along with the sticky grass all these burrs can be good fun to stick on peoples' clothes without them noticing – just, please, keep them out of long hair.

## TEASELS

Teasels are large spiky seed heads that have a very distinct spiral growth pattern. They were historically used for combing hair as well as carding or 'teasing' wool from which it takes its name. The teasel flower is unique in the way that it flowers. They first flower from around the middle of the head and then spread slowly up, towards the tip of the head, at the same time as they spread down towards the base. Because the blooms are quite short-lived the first ring dies off before the rest are formed, it therefore appears as if there are two circles of flowers heading up and down the head. Seeds develop in the head after the flowers are gone and are then dispersed as the head blows around leaving the empty seed head: a stiff, bristly, oval ball.

## CHEW ON SOME GRASS

If you pull a long grass stem out of the sheath of its leaves it has a satisfyingly smooth, pale, juicy end to it; on a hot day or a long walk it can be immensely satisfying to chew on this juicy end flicking its stem with your tongue, to while away the time. If you can combine it with a bit of lying in the grass, watching the world go by or leaning on a gate you can gain the full benefit of grass chewing contemplation.

The humble grass is one of God's rather clever inventions. Humans' global success has relied heavily on the success of grass. Grassland currently covers about a quarter of the earth's surface. It grows in every niche available, right from the very top of the mountains down to the estuary mouth. Our land is held and protected by the instant coverage of grass that acts as an Elastoplast to humans' worst crimes against the land. Every time man causes scars, the land is initially healed over by a swift covering of grass. The grass prevents all the soil from being washed away and, as long as the grass is not cleared away it will increase the soil's fertility. A particularly important feature of grass is that its growth point (meristem) is right down at the base of the plant, at the soil surface. This means that grasses are not killed off by grazing. Nearly all the animals that we eat are herbivores and are fed on grass.

Grass is a very diverse plant with around 160 species represented in the UK alone. Some will tolerate drought, while others thrive in flooded conditions; some can tolerate saline water while others deal well with annual freeze and thaw. This adaptability has enabled them to colonise every niche in the landscape. True grasses include cereals, rice and bamboo as well as the meadow, wayside and lawn grasses. Grasses are typically wind distributed, so don't need brightly coloured flowers to attract insects; but they rely on vast quantities of pollen, which cause a problem to hay fever sufferers, to overcome their

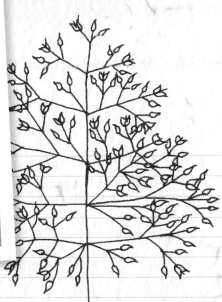

scattergun approach to reproduction. Grasses can be either annual or perennial. Annual grasses grow rapidly, produce large quantities of seed that they distribute and then die off. These are the grasses that rapidly colonise bare soil areas. Perennial grasses grow year in and year out, developing dense roots that are very important for binding soil.

As well as its major use as a source of food and fodder, grass has many uses throughout the world. It is used in the production of paper, roofing, wall construction, clothing, fuel, drinks, basket weaving and many more.

I recently read the cautionary tale of a man whose roll down a hill nearly ended in disaster. He was out walking with friends, on the South Downs, when he was overtaken by a youthful urge to roll down the grass slope along which they were walking. So he did. But as he rolled he started bumping off tussocks and ended up cartwheeling out of control. He landed awkwardly on his neck, which he broke and had to be airlifted off.

I'm not sure what kind of rolling technique he was using and I can only assume the slope was insanely steep. Rolling down a grassy slope is a sure fire way to release your inner child and is something I and my companions must have engaged in several hundred times in my lifetime without any serious ill effects.

## ROLLING SAFELY

There are some points to consider which should help ensure your rolling does not end in disaster. Firstly, you don't need a very steep or long slope at all to enjoy a good roll, so don't be tempted to go off the side of any mountains. Roll like a sausage with your arms stretched above your head or crossed over your chest. Don't try to do forward rolls or roly polys. Before you set off take any sharp, spiky, dangerous, precious or delicate objects from your pockets so you or they don't get damaged or lost. Finally check the slope for any hazards such as sharp rocks, barbed wire, large juicy cowpats or anything else that may be lurking to spoil your fun.

Once you have applied these basic steps of safety you can roll away and giggle 'till your socks drop off.

# Have fun with wild clay

## Linford Bottom, New Forest, May

... We finally had a day today where shafts of sunlight broke through the clouds and showed the spring colours in all their lemon-and-lime glory. The birds have been making a riot all week, zipping from tree to tree without an apparent pause and the brighter weather allowed us to loiter a bit rather than moving everywhere at full speed. While Dunc was setting up the slack-line we found our artistic juices were released and spotting a lovely patch of damp clay we decided to make some sculptures. Grabbing a small handful each we set ourselves the challenge of making a creation on the theme of wildlife. The clay was a perfect consistency and we all enjoyed getting thoroughly orange as we made our creations: some abstract, some with 'philosophical interpretations' or making 'political statements' and some just simple fun. We enjoyed it so much we had to have a second go. As it was close to lunchtime, and the theme for the second round was 'picnics' the alternative interpretations to our work became more and more far fetched as the sugar low kicked in: definitely time for some real food ...

## How to work with wild clay

Much of our countryside has bands of clay running under it and if you are in one of these areas then you are well placed to find your own source of modelling material.

A damp puddle, ditch or stream bank can all provide a rich source of exposed clay but if you can't see any you can try digging through the surface soil and you will often find a good clay substrate, even in your garden. The deeper clays are often finer and contain fewer sticks and stones, so clays exposed lower down the walls of ditches and streams or even around construction sites or road cuttings and sea cliffs, are good places to harvest materials.

The majority of the clay geology and clay soils in this country are situated in the Midlands, south, southeast and northeast of the country, while the uplands of Wales, the southwest and northwest are not the best places to be looking for wild clay. Clays vary hugely depending on the mix of minerals within them. Once you start looking at wild clays and playing with them you will begin to see what a variation in colours and textures clay there is. From the palest greys, to vibrant yellows, oranges and reds, clays come in a whole colour range.

You can tell if you have a good clay soil by rolling a ball between finger and thumb: if you can make a thin ribbon of 5cm or more then you have a good clay. If it is too silty, it will simply squidge but not roll, too sandy and it will crumble and can't be moulded.

Before you start you may need to pick out small stones and sticks and work the clay for a while in your hands to get a nice smooth pliable consistency. If it gets too dry you may need to mix in a little water.

The longer you work, the drier the clay tends to become so access to a puddle or stream can be useful to dampen it down to keep it malleable. If you want to make a damp mixture (known as slip in potting jargon) to stick bits together then you will need to mix a small amount of clay with some water.

## MAKE SCULPTURES AND TILES

Once you get sculpting you really can let your imagination run riot. Free-standing sculptures are great fun and you can incorporate twigs and stones or feathers and shells. Using trees and stones as bases can also add a whole new dimension – grotesque facial parts attached to trees can make the tree spirits come alive. Fashion a ball of clay into a tile and you can make prints of hands and feet or shells and sections of bark – anything that will leave a bold imprint.

## MAKE PINCH POTS

If you want to feel like a real potter or prehistoric housewife why not try to make pots. Pinch pots were the basis of all household storage in Neolithic times. To make a pinch pot, take a handful of clay and work it into a smooth ball. With your fingers cupping the ball start to work your thumbs into the centre to create a well. Slowly squeeze or pinch the clay between thumb and fingers of one hand, while rotating the pot in the palm of the other hand. The pot will slowly grow as the walls are squeezed thinner. Keep going until you have a smooth pot with walls thick enough to hold their shape.

Once you have made your work of art, you can smooth down the surface removing any small cracks with slightly damp hands. The sculpture can then be left to dry. If you leave your pot or sculpture in a plastic bag it will dry out more slowly, to an almost leathery consistency, which is perfect to work on if you wish to decorate the

surface with a sharp twig (spikes from blackthorn, hawthorn or broom all work well for this task). Your clay creation is then ready to be left out to dry fully in the air.

If you find a good source of clay while you are out but can't use your clay there and then you can seal it in to a plastic bag and take it home to play with later. If it dries out a little, just work in some water to revive it.

# Notebook • Clays in the UK

Clays are fine-grained soils which hold water within their network creating their distinct plasticity which allows them to be moulded when wet but becoming rock hard when dry. Clays, geologically, are formed by the erosion of the primary rocks, the finely ground eroded particles are then usually washed away and deposited in some low energy environment such as a lake or shallow sea bed.

Once fired, clays change their physical structure and become a ceramic. Clays therefore have huge potential in their uses as bricks and tiles as well as pottery (earthenware, stoneware and porcelain). The earliest pottery dates back to 14,000 BC and clay tablets were the first writing medium. Balls of clay were used as ammunition and early pipes were made from clay. As well as its continued use in construction and pottery, clays today are used in many industrial processes from paper making and filtering of waste streams to beauty products.

The clay underlying London is known as London clay and just happens to be the perfect medium for tunnelling. In North London the clay lies at the right depth with the ideal thickness for easy tunnelling, enabling the wide underground network that we see today. South of the River Thames the clay deposits run too deep which is why there are not so many underground routes south of the river.

Bricks made from London clay.

Exposed cliff with a layer of London clay

China clay mine at Roche in Cornwall.

Fuller's earth is a clay material that is usually mined from deposits of Lower Greensand in the UK and is used for a variety of purposes, such as removing mineral oils from wool, polishing marble, cat litter and beauty products such as face packs. The main mines were in the Vale of the White Horse in Oxfordshire, south of Bath, Redhill in Surrey and Woburn in Bedfordshire.

China clay or kaolinite is only present in the southwest of England and is currently primarily mined in Devon. Kaolinite is formed by the hydrothermal erosion of the feldspar in granite. The mica and quartz elements of the granite are not eroded so are deposited within the china clay and have to be removed as impurities in the processing of china clay. China clay is so valuable because of its very fine, inert nature and pure white colour. It is primarily used in the paper industry as a filler and in finishing, giving white paper its slight sheen. It is also used in ceramics and cements as a whitening agent and in toothpastes as a non-abrasive polisher.

China clay is used for fine porcelain.

# Sheep's wool and natural dyes

*Glenderamackin, Mungrisedale, Cumbria, October*

... Wow! Today was a wild one. The rain came down sideways as we fought our way up the side of Souther Fell. The squally wind blew clouds of rain in formation across the mountainside – we were just heading over a saddle on the flank of the mountain to reach the hidden valley of Glenderamackin.

Shrouded in our layers of waterproofs, we were 16 mounds of fleece and Gore-tex. Four-year-old Eliza, clinging gamely to Alfie's lead, was propelled up the mountain faster than her little legs could go. The wind rattling our hoods and the steepness of the slope precluded conversation and in the saddle we held tightly to the hands of the smallest members of the family as the older children tried leaning against the wind – there were several moments where it supported their weight before dying down and leaving them stumbling to regain their balance. Over the saddle and dipping down to the stream we were still getting a drenching but the wind was blocked by the great bulk of Blencathra and the sudden silence hummed in our ears. Finally we were able to talk, relax a bit and enjoy the wonderful seclusion of this valley. No sign of human disturbance other than the footpath and a few sheep. Glenderamackin is a perfect v-shaped valley, grass, heather and rock with a white flashing stream along the bottom; a wonderful wild setting only accentuated by the wild weather.

After joining Bannerdale and skirting the northern end of Souther Fell, the yellow glow of the pub lights shone like a beacon guiding us in, towards drying fires and the best pies I know. Beside the track, just by the pub, the sheep, in an effort to avoid the wild weather, were squeezing themselves in against the fence behind the wizened hawthorne hedge. This was clearly a regular hide out and the barbed wire strands were coated by thick skeins of sheep's wool. I took the opportunity to harvest some good sized clumps to add to my dying supplies ...

The hawthorn hedge was clearly a regular hide out and the strands of barbed wire behind it were covered in thick skeins of sheep's wool.

## How to dye wool

In sheep country – particularly moors and mountain areas – there is no shortage of wool caught on blackthorn bushes, barbed wire, heather, even rough rock and dry stone walls. Hunt it out and fill your pockets for a bit of insulation while you walk.

Before you start on the dying process you will need a large old cooking pot, rubber gloves and an old wooden spoon – not only the wool will end up dyed!

### PREPARING THE WOOL

**Wash the wool**  Once you get your wool home you will need to prepare the fibres before you can dye them. Sheep's wool is high in lanolin, a kind of oil that acts as natural waterproofing for the sheep so they do not get waterlogged. If you do not remove the lanolin the colours will just run straight off and not take hold. Washing is most easily done in a large bowl or sink with plenty of warm water and soap or washing up liquid. Give it a good scrub and then rinse well to remove the soap residue as this will interfere with the dying as well. Don't use really hot water to wash the wool otherwise it will turn to felt.

**Soak the wool in fixative**  Next you will need to soak the wool in a fixative if you want your dye to stay permanently; if you are not concerned about permanence you can dispense with this stage. Some colours contain their own fixative, such as tea which is rich in fixative tannins, so if you plan to dye with tannin rich materials you leave out this stage. Of the list below tea, coffee and the oak products really dye permanently while the others will stain and gradually fade away unless you use the fixative.

Vinegar and salt are both good fixatives. You will need 1 part vinegar to 4 parts cold water or 1 part salt to 16 parts water. Vinegar is the better fixative if you are using flowers, leaves and plant parts, while salt is better for fixing fruit dyes.

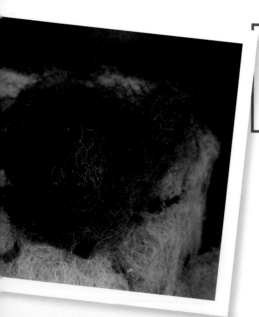

THESE ARE SOME IDEAS TO GET YOU STARTED. REMEMBER THAT SOME PLANTS AND BERRIES ARE POISONOUS SO THE DYE MAY BE ALSO.

## Orange

Alder bark
pomegranate skin
some lichen
carrot roots

## Yellows/browns

walnut hulls
coffee
tea
acorns/oak bark
white onion skins
beetroot
turmeric
rhubarb root

Soak the washed wool in the fixative for an hour and then rinse well before you start dying.

## FINDING NATURAL DYES

To dye the wool it is fun to collect some natural colourants and experiment with the range of colours you can make.

## MAKING THE DYE

With most plant stuffs you will need to chop up the plant material and simmer in about double the volume of water, for around an hour, to release the colour. If after an hour it still looks pale, keep simmering or add more material until you have a good deep colour. Strain out the plant material, leaving just the liquor, before you start dying.

**Dying your wool**  There are two options for a good outcome. Either submerge your wool in the dye and leave it to soak, or, for really good results, leave it overnight to allow the colours to develop more strongly.

Natural dyes work well on pale cotton as well as natural sheep's wool. If you haven't found any sheep wool buy yourself some plain cotton t-shirts and try out some of these dyes at home. Have some fun experimenting with tying elastic bands and string to make tie-dye patterns or just dip the bottom of the t-shirt in for a dip-dye effect. If you are dying cotton t-shirts you can bring the dye and t-shirt mixture slowly to the boil and simmer for around an hour for full colour development without the problem of felting.

Once you have finished dyeing rinse out the excess dye: this may lighten the final colour a shade or so but if the fixative has worked the resultant colour will be permanent.

The colour that results from a dye plant is often not the colour you would expect. The colour is often lighter but also sometimes completely unexpected. For example, beetroot gives a rusty yellow colour while white onionskins can sometimes be quite green. Enjoy experimenting and see which colours work best for you.

## Reds/purples/pinks

red leaves
  sycamore bark
red onion skin
  red berries: strawberries,
raspberries, cherries,
    rosehips, cranberries
avocado skin
rose petals
    red cabbage
    purple berries: elderberries,
blackberries, sloe berries

## Greens

spinach
  nettle
mint
  lichens
  carrot leaves

## Yellow

celery leaves
  dead daffodil flowers
dandelion flowers

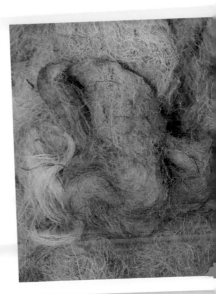

# Notebook • Wool and wealth — how it shaped the UK and beyond

The wool trade has much to answer for in the nature of much of our countryside and our culture too.

There is evidence of woollen cloth production in the UK from the Bronze Age around 1600 BC and even as far back as 10,000 BC in other parts of northern Europe. By the time the Romans invaded there was a well-developed cloth trade that the Romans encouraged. The Saxon invasions in the 5th century nearly destroyed the industry but by the 8th century it had been rebuilt. After the Norman invasion in 1066, trade with Europe increased but it was the export of raw wool in the Middle Ages to the best overseas weavers in Flanders and Italy that really had a big impact in England. From the Lake District, through the Pennines, down to the Cotswolds, West Country, South Downs and across to

East Anglia sheep were farmed and the monarchy became rich on taxing every sack of wool exported. Sheep grazing of vast tracts of land created the form of the countryside as we know it with large areas of moorland, downland and heathland unnaturally devoid of trees and shrubs.

The wool trade was so important in the Middle Ages that people would judge their wealth on the number of sheep they owned. Peasants traded their wool while landowners traded directly with big cloth merchants overseas. The transportation of wool across the country to the ports in Boston, London,

Sandwich and Southampton created many highways and byways still visible today. The church, in particular the large Cistercian monasteries, were involved in the trade and enormous rural churches funded by wool can still be seen throughout dating back to this era. There are fine examples in the villages of Worstead in Norfolk and Lavenham in Suffolk.

Eventually, in the 14th century the monarchy's taxation on the export of the wool became so great that the production of cloth became more profitable. Flemish weavers came to set up business in Norfolk and Suffolk as well as further afield in the Yorkshire Dales and Cumbria.

Throughout the 15th and 16th centuries the wool and cloth trade went from strength to strength. The search for more land for grazing continued and led to the devastating Highland Clearances in Scotland, between 1750 and 1850. Landowners forced tenants off the land which was then converted from arable to sheep farming. The situation was so bad that many Scots fled to the New World, settling on the east coasts of Canada and America.

The city of Leeds was built on the cloth trade and the industrial revolution and mechanisation of processes resulted in the development of canals and railways throughout the country as raw materials had to be shipped in from across the British Empire as far afield as New Zealand and Australia to keep the massive mills running

The wool trade left a truly global footprint but also had a massive impact on the British Isles as we see them today.

*North Downs, late May*

... After a very wet winter, any day without rain feels like a gift that must be appreciated. So today, with the blue sky and scudding white clouds overhead I took Alfie for a walk up on the Downs. Unable to run, with a knee niggle, I decided to use up some excess energy by powering straight up the chalk paths to the meadows above. I arrived at the top, and, with lungs going like bellows and arms akimbo, surveyed the Farrow and Ball patchwork below as the Surrey Weald stretched out almost to the horizon, broken only by the hazy line of the South Downs. Having caught my breath I walked on and, descending some steps, spotted a fluttering on the step below, I bent over to look closer. Alfie came up behind me and I started to caution him, 'no don't', I began... '...Oh!' It was too late, he had stepped right onto the beautiful, plump, wonderfully camouflaged moth. He looked imploringly into my face entirely unaware of his murderous crime as I berated him and lifted his foot. The moth, although apparently dead, was aesthetically undamaged so I scooped it up in my handy poo-cum-collecting bag and took it home for identification and further investigation.

When I reached home I identified my flattened moth as a Poplar Moth. I put the moth in a shoebox on a table in the garden as I looked at it more closely and amazingly it started to flutter around a bit. When I returned later it had gone, either a tasty morsel for one of our garden birds or it had survived. I like to think the latter ...

## How to catch moths

Many moths are night flying insects that are attracted to bright lights. So, choose a dark, mild, still and dry night – cloudy or with no moon. Turn off all house lights and set yourself up with a white sheet and a light source: you want your light source to be the dominant source of light in the area. A powerful torch will work fine. Real moth-ers, mothies or lepidopterists, will use a mercury vapour bulb and even a special trap but the more casual moth observer can have a lot of fun with a white sheet and bright torch on a dark night!

Most moths can't survive the cold winter weather so in the UK they will usually be found flying in the late spring/summer months. Some species will be flying as early as May and keep going to the end of August but the bulk of them will be found in June and July.

Poplar Moth

Cinnabar Moth

Moths

Peppered Moth

Brimstone

Burnet Moth

Angle Shades

So, on your dark summer's night, sitting by your white sheet you will start to attract moths. Records suggest that an average garden can expect to be host to 300 species of moth, so prepare to be overwhelmed. Arm yourself with a good moth book such as Bernard Skinner's *Moths of the British Isles* or Paul Waring's *Field Guide to the Moths of Great Britain and Ireland* or look at Ukmoths.org.uk. Have a few yogurt pots handy and try to pot a moth from your sheet. You can then take your time to identify it. Once you have managed a couple you will start to feel smug but the range of species becomes spellbinding. They have some wonderful names and their shapes and subtleties of colour and tone are captivating.

### DAY-FLYING MOTHS

Not all moths are night flying insects. The Field Studies Council produces a day-flying moths identification guide. Day flying moths can be quite hard to distinguish from butterflies as some of them are quite brightly coloured and patterned. Look out for the red and black Cinnabar moths whose black and orange striped caterpillars feed on the much maligned ragwort plants. Also common and distinctive are the black and red Burnet moths and the orange Clouded Buff.

It can be quite hard to tell the difference between a day-flying moth and a butterfly. The easiest signs are the way they hold their wings – the butterfly folds them together sticking out vertically above their body, while the moth folds them down alongside their body. The butterfly has straight antennae with a club at the end, the moth's antennae are generally curved and with no club end. Sometimes the differences are not easy to spot.

The best places to look for day-flying moths are open heathland and moorland or the wide sunny rides in woodland; around 75 species are found in each of these habitats. Other good places are parks and gardens where 40 species of day moth can be expected.

Any sunny day from late spring to autumn is the time to look, some fly earlier in the season that others but some fly throughout this time.

### HOW TO LOOK AT BUTTERFLIES

We are much more aware of common butterflies due to their more exhibitionist colouring and behaviour in the daytime.

There is some controversy over whether we should still be catching butterflies in nets but it is a good way of seeing them up close. Restrict this to older children and adults as small children may inadvertently damage a butterfly.

On open grassland, butterflies can be caught with pond dipping nets quite easily. The best technique is to wait until the butterfly lands on grass or flowers and then catch it with a very gentle sideways swipe of the net. Do not hit the butterfly with the net rim or damage it in any other way. You can then close the net above it trapping the butterfly inside so you can have a closer look and perhaps take a picture.

You could transfer it in to a jar or plastic container temporarily so you can observe it at leisure but do not shut it in, always return it to the area in which you found them and try to avoid handing them as much as possible.

Orange-tip

Comma

Butterflies

Peacock

Red Admiral

Common Blue

Large Skipper

# Notebook • Ten common night and day moths in UK

Clouded Border

Common Swift

Burnet Moth

Angle Shades

Cinnabar

Peppered Moth

Garden Tiger

Brimstone

Scalloped Oak

# Notebook • Ten common butterflies in the UK

Comma

Common Blue

Meadow Brown

Ringlet

Tortoiseshell

Peacock

Red Admiral

Murbled White

Heath Fritillary

Large Skipper

Orange-tip

# Play with ice

*Dartmoor, November*

... Every hair on my body felt as though it was standing on end as I stepped out onto the moor this morning. Freezing, dry and bright, there was electricity in the air. The sky seemed miles high, a pale duck egg blue with only the finest skeins of combed cirrus; barely visible to the naked eye.

The cold air burnt our lungs as we drew it in and our nose hairs froze but it was absolutely stunning. We threw on as many layers as we could; gloves and buffs leaving as little skin exposed as possible and then rushed out to enjoy the crispness of the frozen morning. Every blade of grass crunched as we walked and every strand of vegetation and wire had a white, crystalline- ruffed coat. Up on the moors the puddles had all been touched by Jack Frost. On some the ice had created a smooth, clear plate but others were elaborately swirled ice discs, patterned, for modesty, like a bathroom window. We could not resist picking up these glass plates; looking at our distorted features through the wild glass and melting holes with our rapidly cooling fingertips. Once we could stand the cold no more we headed home to fill some pots and cutters with water in order to make the most of the next night's freeze and emulating Jack Frost to create our own ice sculptures ...

## How to make ice sculptures

A really good hard frost is quite a treat and is really worth making the most of. Get out early to see the effect of a hoar frost on the countryside before the day warms up and the magic is lost. Everything is silent and seems frozen in time. Rivers, ponds and waterfalls can be very dramatic in an extended cold period. Dead grasses and winter vegetation with its frozen coat can be stunning – particularly if you get a clear blue sky after a cold, cold night.

Ice on puddles and ponds and water containers is irresistible. Melting into it with hands and even some warm water can be a lot of fun and you can create some dramatic sculptures which can then be hung from trees and fences. If you think of it before you go out, take with you a flask of hot water and some metal cutlery and skewers. Once you've found a good sheet of ice, heat the skewers or cutlery in the hot water and melt some holes and patterns in the ice – it is very satisfying!

If you can anticipate freezing temperatures overnight put out some cups full of water and float in a smaller cup. Once frozen you can fit a candle into the central dip and make a beautiful tea light holder.

Get out early to see the effect of a hoar frost on the countryside before the day warms up and the magic is lost. Everything is silent and seems frozen in time.

Try putting out a shallow tray of water and set pastry cutters in it. We put in heart and star shapes and then made holes in them with warmed skewers so they could be hung like ice bunting; they looked really beautiful hanging from bushes outside the window.

To further embellish your ice creations why not put in some flower petals and leaves to make a stained glass window effect.

As long as you wear plenty of warm clothes and gloves you can have loads of fun with ice and its rarity makes it an even more special occasion. Don't forget to come in and warm up slowly with some hot chocolate when you've been out for a while, or even take a flask with you so you can stay out a bit longer!

If you can't wait for a cold snap why not put some trays and cups of water in your freezer right now and have a summer ice party.

# Fun with flowers

Flowers represent the coming of spring and summer and instantly put everyone in a good mood. On a long walk or while relaxing on open grassland there are lots of games that can be played with flowers. Grasslands, heathlands, verges and hedgerows are particularly rich in flowers.

## BUTTERCUPS

Buttercups have a wonderfully glossy, bright yellow upper surface to their petals. On a sunny day the sun reflects off its yellow bowl with a buttery glow. Hold the buttercup flower under someone's chin and if there is a yellow shine on the chin they love butter; if not, they don't ...

## DANDELION CLOCKS

The white globe of the dandelion seed-head may be the scourge of the British gardener but is endlessly entrancing in the wild. When the seeds are ripe the wind disperses them far and wide. On some breezy summer days the air can be speckled with the airborne seeds. Before they have flown you can pick the seed-head stalks and blow the seeds off yourself. The number of blows it takes predicts the time...How many blows will it take? one o'clock, two o'clock, three o'clock ...

## FOXGLOVE FINGERTIPS

We used to love picking the flowers off foxgloves, putting them on our fingertips and tickling each other. Later I discovered that the foxglove is *Digitalis purpurea* the extract of which is used in heart medicines. The flowers, leaves, stem and seeds are toxic and children are told to keep away. If you do handle them, wash your hands carefully and if anyone eats or sucks the flowers, seeds, leaves or stem seek medical attention.

## DAISY CHAINS

The white eyes of daisies dotted over a green field is the epitome of a summer's day. Lazing in the sun on a daisy-strewn field brings out the hippy in all of us. Pick a daisy as near to the ground as possible and make a slit near the end of the stalk by pushing your fingernail through it. Pick another daisy close to the ground and thread the stem through the hole you made in the first stem. Then make a slit in the end of the second daisy's stem, pick another daisy and keep repeating. Before long you will have a daisy chain long enough to make headbands, necklaces, bracelets, belts and you will feel like true flower children.

You don't need to stop at daisies when it comes to making chains, many other flowers can be used as well.

 **He loves me ... He loves me not ...** Once your daisy chain is complete, pick a daisy to find out if the man of your dreams loves you, or not. Pick out a few petals while stating 'he loves me', pull out a few more while stating 'he loves me not'. Work your way around the flower alternating between 'he loves me'... and 'he loves me not' ... the declaration made as you pull out the last pinch of petals gives you your answer ...

## FIND A FOUR-LEAVED CLOVER

While you are enjoying a relaxing sit on the grass collecting daisies for your headband why not keep your eyes open for that elusive four-leaved clover. Most clovers have three leaves but every so often there is a special, very lucky one, with four leaves. If you are lucky enough to find one you are guaranteed to have good luck. The odds are about 10,000 to one that you will find a four-leaved clover but don't let that put you off, there are even more rarely five leaved clovers so you could get super-lucky.

## MAKE A FLOWER PRESS

It is so tempting to pick a flower or two when you're out on a walk, but before long they have wilted and all their beauty is gone. You can preserve their beauty for longer if you press the flowers and they can then be used to make cards and pictures as well. You can buy flower presses

but it is also possible to make your own quite simply. All you need are some good heavy books and some blotting paper.

When you collect your flowers they should be put in water instantly to keep them in good condition. If they have drops of rain or dew remaining on them you must wait for it to dry completely before you attempt to press them or your flowers will go mouldy.

When you get home open your pressing book and place a bit of blotting paper on the page. Arrange your flower or flowers on the page. You can either leave leaves on or take them off, as you wish, fan out petals and make sure neighbouring flowers are not touching. Place a second piece of blotting paper on top making sure the flowers stay in the shape you wish and close the book.

Pile on some other heavy books to make sure the flowers are well and truly pressed. You should try to leave the flowers for a good month before having a look, to give them plenty of time to dry. Fleshy flowers and stems will take longer to dry than delicate ones. Try different flowers and leaves – some work better than others and you will learn as you go.

When you are collecting wild flowers never take more than 10 per cent of the flowers in one area to leave plenty for the bees and only cut the flower – don't pull up the plant as this will kill it and is actually illegal. It is illegal to pick a number of rare, endangered flowers (for example the Lady's Slipper orchid), but the chances are you will not come across any very rare flowers and certainly not ten of them in one place.

If you stick to the 10 per cent rule that there have to be more than 10 flowers before you can pick one, so you should be fine.

Playing with stones

*Yewdale, Lake District, October*

... We had some very reluctant walkers today. It was a grey day, not raining or sunny, not hot or cold, not windy or still – just low on interest with little to commend it. We walked at snail's pace, the children's feet dragging along, barely clearing the rocks on the path, heads down, shoulders slumped until we started going through an old quarry. The sheer slate rock faces drew our eyes up and the occasional tree clinging gamely to the rock face at precarious angles had us all transfixed. Around the quarry there were large heaps of discarded slate rubble, ranging in size from dinner plate down to small shards of pencil-like proportions. They were just too tempting and it took no time at all before Anousha had discovered that she could draw with one piece of slate on another and the walk was transformed. The girls walked along with slate pencils and slate paper, drawing and playing hangman and noughts and crosses – precursors to the digital age tablet and stylus ...

## Games with stones

The countryside you are walking in was formed by the rocky skeleton it overlies. The shape of the ground and the nature of the soils and rivers are all controlled by the underlying geology and that in turn will affect the types of plants that grow and the animals that live there. Keep your eyes on the ground and you may find some interesting stones to have some fun with.

### SLATE
Drawing with stone on stone is a little bit of a miracle that never ceases to please. Slate on slate is the classic combination used in schools in Victorian times. Drawings can be wiped away with a damp cloth and redrawn indefinitely. Slate outcrops are found all the way down the west coast of Britain with quarries primarily found in Cornwall, Wales and the Lake District. Spoil heaps around disused quarries provide plenty of material in all these areas.

### CHALK
Chalk is obviously another great drawing tool that can be found in many chalk geology areas. The purest chalk is the softest, whitest and best for drawing. Small chunks perfect for writing can be found lying on and beside the path in these areas as well as around any scar on the hillside.

### SEARCH FOR FLINT TOOLS
Chalk also contains flints – hard nodules of crystalline quartz. The nodules may be anything from small pebbles to head sized. Their extreme hardness and flaky nature mean they have been used since prehistory as sharp tools. Keep your eyes peeled in chalk and flint areas as it is quite

The countryside you walk in was formed by the rocky skeleton it overlies. The shape of the ground and the nature of the soils and rivers are all controlled by the underlying geology.

possible to find old arrowheads and cutting tools such as hand axes and axe heads, crafted from flint nodules and used by prehistoric man. You can tell if you are in a flint area by looking at the houses and churches in the area: flints are often used as a building material in flint rich areas. Flint and chalk areas predominate in Norfolk and the South Downs stretching from Kent to Wiltshire and beyond.

## TRY YOUR HAND AT FLINT NAPPING

Flint napping is the technique of chipping away at flint to make a useable tool. There is a real skill to napping that requires detailed tuition but just breaking up a flint can result in some seriously sharp flakes of flint that can be used as a basic cutting tool. Have a go at napping your own flints to make your own cutting tool. The easiest way to create a cutting flint is to take a nodule that has already been broken. Secure the nodule, broken side up, on the edge of a rock or board. Start by dulling the sharp edge of the flint with little taps and then hit it with a strong glancing blow at a roughly 90° angle to the sharp edge. Your hammer should ideally be a smoothed granite pebble or other hard smooth rock. You won't have a 100 per cent success rate but eventually you should be able to break off a good chunky flake of flint with really sharp edges. You can then work on this flake to produce the shape of tool you require. Beware of the edges you create – they can be really sharp. See if you can use one to cut through a leaf or piece of paper.

## SEARCH FOR PRECIOUS GEMS

While the UK is not known for its precious gemstone industry there are still sparkly rocks out there to look out for. Young children are always fascinated by crystals and semi-precious rocks such as quartz. Quartz is estimated to make up 12 per cent of the earth's crust. In granite areas quartz is widespread, it may form thick bands in the rock that shatter and become scattered along paths. Quartz is one of the elements making up granite and continental igneous rocks, but can also be found in sandstone. Oceanic volcanic rocks have very little quartz and limestone and chalk will have virtually none. Look out for it wherever you are and you will almost certainly find some. Quartz is typically clear and glass-like, it breaks into hexagonal shapes and is very hard, hard enough to scratch glass. It is also used as the timekeeping element in quartz watches. Clear quartz is commonly found, less often it can be found coloured white, known as milky quartz, pink, known as rose quartz, and purple, known as amethyst.

## FINDING SHAPES IN THE STONES

Interesting shaped stones are always good fun and when you start looking I can guarantee that it will be just minutes before someone picks one up and starts shooting with it like a gun. We have collections of 'mutant' stones – one shaped like a seal and another like a mushroom are looking at me right now. You can also play the alphabet game with the rocks and stones on the path – find stones and fissures shaped like letters of the alphabet.

## GAMES WITH STONES

**Jacks** Jacks, also known as knucklebones, is a game that dates back a very long way. The games

four stones on the ground and holds the fifth in their hand. The stone in the hand is thrown into the air, while in the air the player must pick up just one of the other stones before catching the stone again. This is all done with just one hand. If this is completed successfully the second step is to put the picked up stone down again and this time, holding one stone in the hand throw it into the air. While it is in the air, this time, pick up two stones so you have two in the hand and catch the one in the air so you have three in your hand. Repeat this picking up the three stones and four stones in the last two goes. You can decide whether you are allowed to sweep before you pick up multiple stones or if they have to be picked individually.

**Riding the elephant** The second game is also known as 'riding the elephant'. In this game you start with one stone, throw it in the air and try to catch it on the back of your hand. If you are successful throw it off the back of the hand and catch it in your palm again. If you manage that pick up a second stone and throw them both in the air and catch them both on the back of the hand, again if successful throw them off the back of the hand and catch on the palm. Repeat this until you can throw all five, catch them on the back of the hand and then toss them and catch them in the palm. A variation on this game is that you throw all the stones in the air and catch as many as you can on the back of the hand. The number you catch counts as your score. The next person has a turn to get their score. You can either play first to a certain number or a set number of rounds and the person with the highest score wins.

require each player to start with five knuckle sized stones or pebbles. Apparently there are many variations on this game but these are the two games that I play.

**Peas in the pod** The first game is sometimes known as 'peas in the pod'. The first player puts

Let's go fly a kite

*Reigate, Surrey*

... We were all very excited because we had arranged a last minute skiing holiday. We would drive over to the Alps and stay with some friends in their chalet, have five days skiing and then stop off in Paris on our way home for the twins' birthday. We have never driven to skiing or been to Paris before so it was to be a bit of a double adventure.

As I was packing I put all passports, driving licences, EHIC cards, travel insurance documents into our travel folder. I flicked through each of the passports and ... yes, you've guessed it the twins' passports were out of date and I hadn't even realised! All options to get round this inescapable fact were pursued and dropped, we had to accept there was no skiing holiday this year. After a few hours of sulking and extreme grumpiness we found that our most gorgeous and lovely friends in the Lake District were at home and receiving guests. We packed up the car and headed north instead of south.

While there we climbed the snowy heights of Lakeland and while we didn't get any skiing we did have a lot of fun with some kites on a sunny, blowy, icy cold day ...

## How to make your own kite

The weather in this country can be unpredictable but flying kites can be done almost everywhere in the countryside whether that is mountain, moorland, downland, common land or park. It is very satisfying to successfully launch a kite and there are many different kites available. We have pocket kites that fit into a small purse for those impromptu kite-flying sessions but we also have a big 2m wing paraglider style kite which we bought after our great day out at the top of a mountain in the Lakes. Other friends have stunt kites that they can show off their clever tricks with but I have only ever mastered a bit of swooshing around before crashing to the ground scaring the living daylights out of anyone in the vicinity. You can make your own kite very easily.

Although very simple this is probably a task to do before you go out on your kite-flying trip. You will need a heavy-duty bin bag, 2m of 5mm dowel, 10m string and a short sturdy stick.

● Using a heavy-duty bin bag – garden waste bags are ideal – cut a diamond shape 1m long and 1m wide crossing at 25cm from one end.
● Cut two 1m lengths of 5mm dowel and join them to the plastic with duck tape at each corner of your diamond shape.

The weather in the UK can be unpredictable but flying kites can be done almost everywhere in the country whether that is mountain, moorland, downland, common land or park

● Where the dowels cross in the middle make two small holes in the plastic and push your string through one hole and back through the other and tie around the dowels.

● Finally cut strips of plastic from the bag remains to make a tail. The tail should be about 5cm wide and five times longer than the kite – in this case 5m long. Tie the tail on to the base of the dowel and you are ready to fly.

● Wind the string around a sturdy stick so you have something to hold without cutting your hands on the string.

## NOW GO FLY YOUR KITE

This kite will fly in light to moderate but not very strong winds. The ideal day can be identified by the whispering of wind in the leaves, but not the thrashing of the branches. Stand with your back to the wind, get someone to hold the kite at chest height, hold the string taut and step back into the wind as the kite is released; it should fly. If the wind is light at ground level you may need to run back to get the kite in the air and hope there is more wind higher up.

# Games for walking

## Andringitra National Park, Madagascar

... Andringitra is Madagascar's answer to Yosemite in the western USA. There is even a 'Half Dome-like' rock slab mountain (Tsaranoro Peak) looming over our campsite. The main difference is that there is no one here. With only three camps in Tsaranoro valley there are probably only about 30 tourists in an area the size of Snowdonia. Only ourselves and the staff are at our camp so we haven't seen any other visitors yet. While we are here we are keen to get up high and go on a long day hike and our target is the top of the 'Half Dome' Tsaranoro Peak. We need to take a guide and they are very sceptical about us taking Lottie, who is only seven, on this 10-hour hike. We eventually decide to give it a go and set off early with our guide and a helper carrying food and water to keep us going.

Initially we are in the burnt brown scrub and red dust of the valley but soon we start to climb steeply up, out onto the rough granite rocks. It is not long before Lottie is beginning to flag. I can see the guide raising his eyes to the heavens and giving us 'I told you so' kind of looks as we stop for our first biscuit break about half an hour from camp. I begin the usual distractions and anticipate a day of jollying and cajoling. Poppy and Thea are beginning to worry that we will be benighted on the mountain if we don't keep our pace up – and they've heard there are some steep ridges on the descent. They start asking Lottie questions about My Little Pony, her current obsession on which she has a Mastermind-like knowledge. As soon as her mouth starts working Lottie's legs seem to go into overdrive. Every so often Poppy or Thea throw in a question and she's off again. Legs and mouth don't stop for six hours.

The guide can't believe what he is seeing and we reach the summit in time for lunch with buzzards circling above our heads and the country laid out below our feet like a bedspread ...

## Games to keep the legs moving

If you want a happy, long walk with children, then some kind of distraction is usually required. Friends, cousins or someone of around their own age is often the best solution, a dog is a great distraction but if none of these things are available there are lots of great games, that still allow or even require forward movement that can be called in to help. Some require lots of input but the ones that get the children talking and

thinking are the best and give you time to enjoy your surroundings as well as the company.

## TELLING STORIES

We often tell each other stories. There are lots of ways of doing this: two word stories where each player just has two words to progress the story; Fortunately/fortunately where each player takes it in turn to add to the story but has to start their bit alternately with fortunately or unfortunately so the story lurches from one improbable disaster to the next, interspersed with improbable solutions.

Or, you can just make up stories. If you are inventive and have infinite story telling resources to hand you will be fine but if like me your mind freezes at the demand for a story you can ask your

audience to help. Get them to choose the setting for the story; they can set the main characters and their names. You can ask them to pick out a couple of objects that must appear in the story and even a situation or challenge that may arrive. Whenever you get stuck just ask them to provide the next problem or solution, new character or whatever you need to keep the story going; in this way stories can grow and develop for quite lengthy walks and often inspire the listeners to start their own story, while you have a rest.

## QUIZZES

Our children have always loved quizzes. If you know what books they have been reading, films or TV shows they have been watching, or subjects they have been learning about at school these are all good starting points for questions. Maths challenges always seem to go down well, as well as questions about family members or general knowledge. Just have a look around you for some more inspiration, quizzes can be a great way to get them interested in their surroundings too ... What kind of tree grows acorns? Which character in *Winnie the Pooh* liked to eat acorns? If a squirrel collected 10 acorns and a Jay stole five how many would there be left? There is no end to the questions you can ask.

Let the children ask questions. Almost like truth or dare, each child is allowed to ask each adult three questions and the adults have to answer the questions as honestly as they can (or are prepared to).

### HAND SQUEEZE MATHS

My children love to play this with Duncan and now they often play it together. You just hold hands and one person is the hand squeezer and the other the mathematician. The hand squeezer gives the other person a series of hand squeezes. A short squeeze counts as five, a long squeeze as 10. You can change the numbers to suit the age and mathematical ability of the children; it could be one and two or three and six or any other combination of numbers. The length of the squeeze series and the speed with which they are delivered all depend on how hard you want the challenge to be. If they are getting a bit too good make them start from 100 and minus the hand squeezes. Remember you need to work out the number you have reached as well so you can check their answer at the end.

### LEAD ME

Another hand holding game; this requires a certain amount of trust. Some children love it and some hate it but get them to walk with their eyes closed as you lead them. You will need to warn them about encroaching bushes and nettles, roots, logs and branches on the path, muddy puddles and so on. The only trouble with this game is they usually want to reciprocate and do you trust them to lead you?

### SINGING SONGS

Singing songs is always a great distraction. Children's songs tend to have a good rhythm and make good marching songs. Make sure you have a good repertoire and know the words or you could find yourself going crazy repeating the same line ad infinitum. Counting songs can go on

for ages, for example: 'The Twelve Days of Christmas, One Man Went to Mow, Found a Peanut, The Quartermaster's Stores, Ten Green Bottles, Alice the Camel. These songs all go on and can drive you crazy after a while but it can be good fun thinking up new lyrics. Make a note of a few different songs before you go if you struggle to remember them so you don't get stuck on the same one for too long. My older kids like to sing pop songs with each of them taking on a different role; one is the lead singer, another is the drums, another the dancer and another the backing singer ... depending on how many roles are needed.

## PLAY WITH WORDS

There are many word games and challenges you can employ as you walk a few more ideas include: One person says a word and the other one has to come up with the opposite – black:white; bright;dim; up:down and so on.

Think of some cockney rhyming slang and then make up your own rhyming slang.

Think of two letters for a word beginning for example 'de' and come up with as many words as you can with those two letters at the start, they can be as easy or hard as you like e.g. dead, desert, despicable – see how long a list you can get and the longest word you can find.

be
curious

*Reigate Priory School, Reigate*

... When I arrived at school today it looked like a crime scene from a mass murder. The playground was covered in chalk outlines of bodies in grotesque poses. The girls dragged me across the playground to look at some of the chalk bodies. Through their excited jabbering I discovered that they had been learning about the sun and throughout the day they had been out in the playground drawing around the shadow of their 'gnomonic' friends. It transpired that the gnomon is the device at the centre of a sundial that casts its shadow. They had made a human sundial using their friend as a gnomon and they drew around her shadow every hour throughout the school day. This revelation of the sun and shadows and the telling of time had clearly entranced them and they talked about it for the whole journey home, oblivious to their usual need for food ...

## How to understand the sun

The basis of all navigation relies on an understanding of time and that requires a detailed knowledge of our relationship with the sun.

Once you have mastered the understanding that we (on the earth) are spinning on our axis at a predictable speed and that we circle the sun equally predictably, then you can have all kinds of fun playing with the sun and its trajectory over the ground. The downside of all these clever tricks and investigations is that they require the sun to be visible. The ability to see the sun in this country is a lot less predictable than our rotations.

### FIND NORTH AND SOUTH

You need to stay in one area for a good length of time – preferably all day – to be able to do this activity. You also need an area of ground that is open to the sun and can stay undisturbed, a garden, park, open grassland, beach would all work.

Collect several finger diameter sticks and, in an open bit of ground, plant one of your sticks. This stick is your gnomon and is the centre of your sundial. This gnomon stick will cast a shadow on the ground, so plant another stick at the end of the shadow. Return every so often throughout the day, ideally until the sun goes down, look to see where the shadow has moved and plant another stick at the shadow's tip. If the ground is too hard or there are no sticks, you could use stones or anything else you fancy to mark the end of the shadow at each visit.

By the end of the day you will have a curved line progressing alongside your gnomon stick. The line you have created will tell you where south and north are. If you drew a line from your gnomon stick to the very closest point of the shadow line it would be pointing directly

The basis of all navigation relies
on an understanding of time and
that requires a detailed knowledge
of our relationship with the sun.

north–south. Your shadow would have reached this point at exactly mid-day – not 12:00 but the point where the sun reached its highest point (apogee) in the sky and was about to start going down – half way between sunrise and sunset. You can tell which end of the line points north because if you are north of the Tropic of Cancer (as we are in Britain) your gnomon stick will be to the south of the shadow line. The notebook section on page 106 should explain why.

## WHERE WILL THE SUN SET? FIND EAST AND WEST

If you don't have time to sit around all day trying to find which direction is north you can do a quicker but slightly less accurate measurement to work out which way is east and west. As before, plant your gnomic stick and mark the end of the shadow. This time you only have to wait 15 minutes or so before you come back, look for the end of the new shadow and make a second mark. Once you have two marks join these with a line and this line should point roughly east–west from which you can draw a perpendicular line to establish north and south. For real accuracy the shadows used to measure your east–west line should be of equal length i.e. there should be equal amounts of time before and after midday, however, if you want a rough idea and you are somewhere around the middle of the day then this will be good enough.

Don't be fooled into thinking that just because you have identified the west that you will be facing the right way when the sun sets. It is a common misconception that the sun rises in the east and sets in the west. If you are around one of the equinoxes in March and September then the sun will indeed be setting in the west, however, if you are nearer one of the solstices then you could be looking in quite the wrong direction. Towards the summer solstice, June in the northern hemisphere, the sun rises north of east and sets north of west. Conversely towards the

winter solstice, December in the northern hemisphere, the sun rises south of east and sets south of west. At the equator the greatest movement between extremes of sunset will be 23.5° but the further you move away from the equator the greater this difference. This can be significant if you return to watch your perfect sunset off the coast of Cornwall. Imagine that the first time that you watched the sunset was in June and you decide to return in December all bundled up and cosy with a glass of champagne.

The sun will set some 90° before it reaches your anticipated setting point – just over your left shoulder and quite possibly out of sight! As a rough guide, on midsummer's eve in the UK the sun sets almost at northwest and in midwinter it sets at southwest.

If you want to watch the sunrise then it rises in the northeast on midsummer's day, in the east at the equinoxes and in the southeast on midwinter's day.

### HOW LONG UNTIL SUNSET?

You are rushing to watch the perfect sunset and the sun is falling fast. How long do you have to get to your viewing point?

We know that our planet makes a complete 360° revolution every 24 hours. This means is turns through 15° every hour or 0.25° every minute. As a rough guide, with an open view of the horizon the sun drops about a finger width in five minutes. So hold your hand up sideways, at arms length, to the horizon and measure how many finger widths between sun and horizon. You have five minutes for every finger before the sun starts to set.

# Notebook ·
# Understanding our solar system

The relationship between the sun and the earth is a very hard concept to really believe. Like sitting in a stationary car while another moves slowly off, even when we know that the earth is moving and the sun is stationary, it really doesn't feel like it. Every molecule in our body is telling us that we are sitting quite stationary, on a very solid and stationary bit of ground as we sit and watch the sun clearly rise. Similarly when we watch a sunset from a solid piece of land we can clearly see the sun falling in the sky. As it crosses the horizon the movement is entirely tangible from one moment to the next, it is clearly falling. But no.

As far back as 250 BC a dissenter, Aristarchus of Samos (a clever Greek), suggested that the sun was at the centre of our solar system and that it could be the earth that was doing the moving. Copernicus famously took on this idea and controversially published his theory of the earth spinning on its axis and orbiting the sun just before he died in 1543. Galileo further progressed these theories and ended up under house arrest, at the hands of the Catholic Church, for his pains. The modern view of the solar system was more or less in place by 1727 following major inputs from Johannes Kepler and Sir Isaac Newton.

We now have a full understanding of how the earth rotates on its axis once every 24 hours giving us our day and night cycle. We also understand that the earth takes 365 days to orbit the sun giving us our year. This gives us our basic understanding of time. Further subtleties in the system are introduced by the fact that the earth is tilted at an angle of 23.5° off vertical as it circles the sun. This means that at the June solstice the northern hemisphere is tilted towards the sun, which is directly over the Tropic of Cancer (23.5°N). At the December solstice the southern hemisphere is tilted towards the sun which is directly over the Tropic of Capricorn (23.5°N).

Cancer is the sign of the zodiac for the month from mid summer in the Northern Hemisphere (22 June to 22 July), when the sun is directly over the Tropic of Cancer. Capricorn is the zodiac sign for when the sun is over the Tropic of Capricorn (22 December to 22 January). This may help you remember which tropic is to the north and which to the south of the equator. The Arctic and Antarctic circles are those places on earth where daylight can be almost constant or almost absent when the sun is over either one of the tropics, the circles extend to 23.5° from the nearest pole.

Between the solstices are the spring
(March) and autumn (September) equinoxes.
These are the days when the sun is directly
over the equator and the whole earth
experiences days and nights of equal length;
the word equinox comes from Latin roots and
literally means *equi* – equal, *nox*　night.

　　The angle that we are tilted at is crucial for
the wildlife on our planet and the seasonal
cycles that we experience. If there were no tilt
there would be no seasons and if the tilt was
greater we would suffer such extremes of
temperature that the planet would be
uninhabitable.

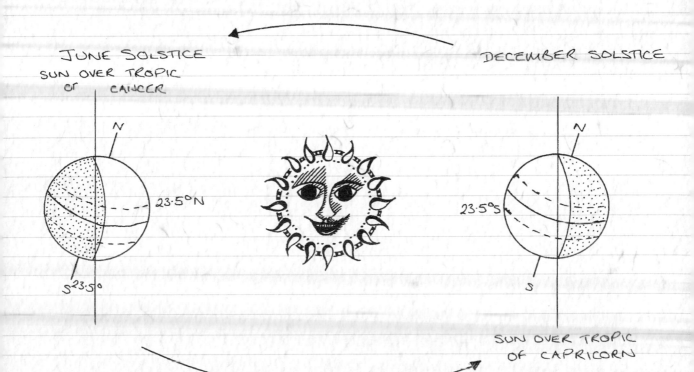

JUNE SOLSTICE
SUN OVER TROPIC
of　CANCER

DECEMBER SOLSTICE

N

23.5°N

S 23.5°

N

23.5°S

S

SUN OVER TROPIC
OF CAPRICORN

Wild flower spotting

*Norbury Park, Surrey, June*

... On our walk today we decided to count how many different colours we could see. The greens and browns were pretty much covered at first glance as we set off through the wood and then we stepped out into an area of open grassland. It was a knee-high sea of swaying grasses with a polka dot appliqué of colour. The most obvious were the yellow buttercups and dandelions contrasting beautifully with the greens but as we walked we were treated to pinks and purples, oranges, reds, whites and blues – we had barely gone more than a couple of hundred metres before we had made a whole rainbow ...

## Do a wildflower count

The seasons in the open countryside provide a rolling rainbow of colours in the flowers as they come into and out of flower. Why not have a closer look at the flowers as you walk and really enjoy the variety in the colours and structures you can find. There may be many more flowers than you had ever imagined.

The flowers you see in different habitats will vary quite considerably and if you get very keen you can get involved in the national wildflower count. This is organised by Plantlife (an organisation that champions plant life in the UK) and you can register on their website as a wildflower counter. At the most basic level you devise a 1km walk in your 1km square and using their list of 20–30 wildflowers for your particular habitat you simply record the species that you see on your list. If you want to get further involved there are more complex counts you can make right up to a full inventory of every plant you can identify within five plots of your 1km square.

### FLOWERS IN DIFFERENT HABITATS
In hedgerows and verges around the country you can often see **cow parsley**, white and red **Dead Nettle**, pink **Herb Robert**, **Red Campion**, **Toadflax** and **poppies**.

**CHALK GRASSLAND**   Found primarily on the North and South Downs in England the grassland is typically managed with sheep grazing so is often close cropped and the flowers are tight to the grassy floor. Typical flowers include: **buttercup** species, **Hairy Violet**, **Red Clover**, **Knapweed**, **cowslip**, **Kidney Vetch** and several **orchid** species. The harsh conditions for flowers on chalk grassland mean that no single species can dominate and results in its typically species rich/high diversity habitat with a large number of species none of which have high coverage.

**PASTURES AND MEADOWS**  In pastures and meadows that have been allowed to go to flower you may find **daisies**, **buttercups**, **Red Clover**, **Tufted Vetch**, **Meadowsweet**, **Field Scabious**, **Yellow Iris**.

Why not have a closer look at the flowers as you walk and really enjoy the variety in the colours and structures you can find. There may be many more varieties of flowers than you had ever imagined.

**ACID GRASSLAND**, which is usually found overlying sands and gravels in heath areas such as the Brecklands, the New Forest, on the Welsh/English border in Shropshire, The Weald and Coast of southwest England. Because of its nutrient-poor soils acid grassland is low in numbers of flowers, and the variety of species is poor in general. Where there are flowers typical varieties will include the **yellow broom** and **gorse**, **foxgloves** and **Tormentil**.

**LOWLAND HEATHS** contain such flowering plants as **heathers**, **broom**, **foxgloves** as well as some **orchids**.

**HEATHLANDS** in the mountains are dominated by **heathers** that provide shadows of purples when in flower. You can see a wide range of heathers as you cross the mountainous areas of the Lake District, Wales and Scotland including **bell heathers** and **ling**; the other splash of colour

comes from the autumn berries of **bilberries, crowberries, cow berries** and **bearberry**.

**MOUNTAIN MEADOWS** support arctic alpines such as: Purple Saxifrage, Moss Campion, Alpine Cinquefoil, mountain avens, Alpine Lady's Mantle, Alpine Catchfly and Alpine Mouse-ear. On richer soil you may find alpine hay meadow flowers like Wood Crane's-bill, Globeflower, Water Avens, Wild Angelica and Roseroot.

# Hawks and falcons

*Grande route, Pyrenees, August*

... We drove the car to the top of the ridge on the Grande Route Pyrenean and then Caroline and I ran along the ridge to end up in Arles Sur Tech. It was a beautiful run along dry footpaths, weaving our way between rocks and bushes. As we ran, the low scrub scratched at our ankles and the scent of thyme wafted around us as we dodged and danced our way up and down along the narrow path. We could see for miles across the foothills and out to the plains below. We were enjoying the cooling breeze in our faces, which made the heat of the morning bearable, when the path took us around a large rock outcrop. Caroline was in front and stopped suddenly without saying a word and I collided with her but saw instantly what had caused the abruptness and silence. Just ten metres away standing on a rock was an enormous, majestic Golden Eagle. Our sudden arrival had interrupted his surveying of his vast domain; he turned a yellow eye on us and, fixing us with a jaundiced stare, launched into the void below. His wings seemed to go on forever as he stretched them out to take to the air. It was effortless and instantaneous and all we could do was stand and revel in his majesty. We watched, mouths open, as he soared off the side of the mountain, utterly relaxed and in charge ...

## Watching birds of prey

I have only seen wild Golden Eagles once before and that was in the highlands of Scotland and we were some distance away. Every sighting of a bird of prey is a treat and seems like a privilege. They are undoubtedly the royalty of the skies and honour us with their presence.

Birds of prey have suffered greatly at the hands of humans in Britain, their numbers reaching an all time low during the 1950s and 60s. The main threats came from three directions: in hunting and shooting areas gamekeepers killed the birds as they posed a threat to the game they were trying to raise; in lowland areas habitat loss made suitable food and good roosts less available; and the introduction of the pesticide DDT had a devastating effect on these birds.

DDT was an insecticide used in the Second World War to control malaria and typhus amongst the troops. After the war its use accelerated in agriculture to control insect pests; unfortunately the insects were also a food source for birds which accumulated the DDT in their tissues and in turn become food for the birds of prey further concentrating the DDT load. Although not fatal to

Every sighting of a bird of prey is a treat and seems like a privilege. They are undoubtedly the royalty of the skies and honour us with their presence.

the birds at the top of the food chain, their eggshells were affected and eventually became so weak that they lost virtually all their young and their numbers plummeted. DDT was finally banned in the UK in 1984. The banning of DDT along with raised awareness amongst gamekeepers and work on habitats has resulted in a significant recovery in numbers of most bird of prey species over the last 30 years.

## HOW TO TELL THE DIFFERENCE BETWEEN A FALCON AND A HAWK

The day flying birds of prey in the UK are divided between the falcons and the hawks but how can you tell which is a falcon and which is a hawk? It is not that easy, particularly as our view of a bird of prey is often limited to a distant sighting or a momentary glimpse. There are some features to look out for to differentiate between them.

**THE WINGS** Falcons have long slender wings, pointed at the end while hawks' wings are more rounded. The larger hawks have individual feathers visible along the outer rear edge looking almost like fingers.

**THE FLIGHT PATTERN** As falcons have thinner wings they have a more rapid wing beat, with

Kestrel

Sparrowhawk

only short periods of gliding. Hawks have a slower wing beat and more frequent and longer duration periods of gliding. Both hawks and falcons are distinguishable from other birds when they fly as they often glide and soar with their wings held in a shallow 'V' shape.

**THE HEAD SHAPE**, which can sometimes be seen while the birds are perched. A falcon's head is shorter and rounded while a hawk's is sleek and pointed.

## SEEING NATIVE HAWKS

There are ten hawks that may be seen in the UK but three of them are vanishingly rare and only three are regularly seen, apart from in very localised breeding spots of the UK.

**BUZZARD** The UK's most common bird of prey with an estimated 79,000 breeding pairs it is resident throughout the UK so can be seen year round with winter grounds in the east. It is most likely to be seen over wooded hillsides and perched on posts and is most numerous in the wilder areas of south-west England, Wales, Lake District and Scotland but present everywhere, even occasionally in towns.

**SPARROWHAWK** There are around 35,000 resident pairs throughout England, Wales, Scotland and Ireland. It is a small hawk that uses its manoeuvrability to hunt for small birds in woodland and gardens. You will often be alerted to their presence by the warning by the cry of small birds.

**RED KITE** With 1,600 pairs now recorded the Red Kite is a conservation success story. Successful reintroduction programmes now see strong year round populations in many central and northern

Hen Harrier

England counties as well as much of central Scotland and central Wales where they managed to hang on through all the persecution. Numbers of Red Kites have increased so dramatically that in a single trip along the M40 it is quite feasible to count up to 40 individuals in an hour.

**THE GOLDEN EAGLE, GOSHAWK, HEN HARRIER AND MARSH HARRIER** are not widely seen but have significant populations in some locations.

**Golden Eagles** can be seen year round in the northwest of Scotland over the mountains and islands and on the RSPB Haweswater reserve in Cumbria.

Common Buzzard

**Goshawks** are resident year round in Wales, midland England, northern Scotland and the borders. It is usually seen around woodlands and open countryside, it is most visible in winter when display flights bring it out in to the open.

**Hen Harriers** can be seen in winter in the valleys, fenland and coastal areas of southwest, south and southeast England and south Wales. In summer they prefer open heath and moorland and can be seen in North Wales, the Pennines, the Scottish Borders and northern Scotland. They are usually seen flying low looking for voles and small mammals. They are highly persecuted in grouse shoot areas and earned their name by hunting in hen houses.

**Marsh Harriers** are the largest of the harriers. They are resident in a very restricted area of Kent with localised summer breeding areas on the coast mostly in East Anglia and south coast with a few pairs in northeast England and the southwest. They are seen over reed beds and marshes, in breeding areas, between April and October.

**THE HONEY BUZZARD, MONTAGU'S HARRIER AND WHITE TAILED EAGLE** are all extremely rare in the UK. The Honey Buzzard and Montagu's Harrier are summer breeding visitors from Africa with just a handful of breeding pairs each. Their breeding sites are heavily protected but the RSPB has wardened watch points for Honey Buzzards.

**The White Tailed Eagle** is the largest and most rare of the resident UK birds of prey. It is resident in the extreme north west of Scotland on the

Peregrine Falcon

Merlin

Goshawk

Hobby

coast and offshore islands where it has been reintroduced following extinction due to persecution.

## SEEING NATIVE FALCONS

There are four falcons seen in this country.

**KESTREL** With 46,000 pairs the Kestrel is probably the most easily recognised of the falcons. With its long pointed wings it is often seen hovering alongside roads keeping its eyes peeled for small mammals in the verges. They can be seen year round throughout the British countryside although not in woodlands, mountains or treeless wetlands.

**PEREGRINE FALCONS** With 1,500 breeding pairs these are the largest and fastest of our resident falcons and often used in hawk flying displays to show off their impressive speed and agility. In the summer they breed in rocky cliffs in the mountains and sea cliffs of the west, southwest and north of England. They move to the lowlands in winter – coastal areas of south and southeast England as well as the Welsh/English borders.

**MERLIN** A small falcon with 900 to 1,500 breeding pairs it breeds on open moorland, spending the summer months April to September in southwest England, Wales, northern England and Scotland. In winter (October to April) they come down to lower ground and can be found over much of lowland England.

**HOBBY** There are 900–1,500 breeding pairs and it can be seen between April to October throughout England and just into southern Wales and southern Scotland. It favours quarries and open heathland. In the winter months they move to inland and lowland areas with many more visitors from Iceland.

Marsh Harrier

# Notebook • Man and hawk – falconry, the sport of kings

There is a long history of a hunting relationship between humans and birds. The earliest references are in Mesopotamia and date back to 2,000 BC. From then on falconry centred on the regions of Mongolia and central Asia and it is believed that the sport was introduced to Europe around 400 BC when the Huns and Alans invaded from the east. It was around this time that it was also introduced to Japan from China. Falconry was a symbol of high status throughout the Middle East and the Mongolian Empire as well as medieval Europe and Japan. Meat caught by falcons was considered halal which encouraged the use of falconry in Islamic cultures.

Large amounts of time, money and space were required to train a falcon limiting the sport to the noble classes. A high ranking noble would have his own mews and would employ falconers to train their birds which would then be flown as sport. The young birds and eggs were hard to acquire and very expensive; they would sometimes be given as valuable gifts between visiting nobles and royalty. Some royals were particularly fond of falconry: it is reputed that Henry VIII's mews were more extensive than his stables and Mary Queen of Scots enjoyed flying Merlins.

The joy in watching falconry is the bond of teamwork between man and bird but also the pleasure in watching at close quarters the amazing flying prowess and extreme skills of the hunting bird.

Falconry reached its height in the 17th century after which, with the development of firearms, noble sport moved to hunting with the gun. There was a resurgence of falconry in the UK in the late 19th and early 20th centuries when the development of transmitters increased the lifespan of a falcon and made it easier to track and retain them. Falconry is still practised today in the UK commonly as a demonstration sport at displays but falcons are also flown to keep runways, city squares and the Centre Court at Wimbledon free of pigeons. Falconry remains an important part of the Arab, Kyrgyz and Japanese heritage and culture.

**Take a look at the fields as you travel through the countryside. The story of fields is really about their enclosure. Without walls, hedges and fences there are no fields. In the UK each region has very distinct field boundaries dictated by the materials that were readily available, the purposes to which the field boundary was being put and regional styles that developed over the years. There have also been changes in fashion over time.**

Each era had their own reasons and criteria for putting in field boundaries and they would also have developed their own techniques to create a boundary to suit their needs. If you look at fields today it is possible to see the remnants of field boundaries demonstrating many different techniques within one region and most particularly between regions.

Fields were formed for various reasons. The boundary may have been nothing more than a row of markers to show the extent of one person's land. More robust boundaries were developed for containing livestock. Before stock proof fencing livestock would have needed constant supervision from a shepherd or stockman to stop the animals from wandering off and to protect them from predators. There were many other reasons to plant hedges, including: to show rights of way alongside tracks or to provide shelter, they were sometimes planted as a source of wood or fruit and herbs or even additional animal fodder. All these purposes could accommodate a less robust boundary than the continuous stock proof boundary required for stock control.

So if field boundaries have been around since the Bronze Age is there any way of knowing how old a particular one is?

## HOW TO TELL THE AGE OF HEDGES AND WALLS:

**HEDGES** You can have a good go at estimating the age of a hedge by counting the number of tree and hedge species in a 30-yard length of hedge. This technique was devised by Max Hooper in the 1970s and says that the age of the hedge in centuries is equal to the number of species of trees and shrubs in a 30-yard stretch of hedge.

It is not necessary to have an encyclopaedic knowledge of tree and shrub species, just to be able to differentiate between them. Measure or pace out your 30 yards (around 27 metres). Then systematically work your way along your length of hedge tallying down each new species of shrub or tree as you go. Once you reach the end of your 30 yards add up the number of tree and shrub species you counted. Five species would suggest a hedge planted 500 years ago (during the Wars of the Roses), seven species 700 years ago (a medieval hedge) and so on...

While not completely fool proof this technique works well for hedges up to around 1,500 years old. The really ancient hedges of Anglo-Saxon and Roman origin are hard to differentiate from one another, presumably there comes a time where the maximum diversity for a hedgerow is reached. Other than the very ancient hedgerows there are some other instances where relying on tree and shrub species is unreliable. Elm in hedges, as in woodland, deters other species so the small number of trees and shrubs may be misleading. The hedge may be older than it appears. Conversely a new hedge adjoining an

If you look at fields today it is possible to see the remnants of old field boundaries, demonstrating many different techniques within one region and most particularly between regions.

**WALLS** Every stone-bearing district has its own style of stone-walling. Stones were invariably used from the fields themselves and often had the purpose of clearing the land of stones that could result in very thick stone walls in some areas.

If there is lichen growing on your stone wall then it is quite likely the lichen has been living there since the time the wall was first built. It is possible to age stone walls from the lichen growing on them. Certain lichens grow at a very consistent rate and make it easy to calculate how old they are and hence how old your wall is. This is a science known as lichenometry.

The first job is to calibrate your lichen. Lichens grow at different rates in different areas dependent on levels of air pollution and prevailing weather conditions. The best place to check growth rates is on gravestones. The burial date on a gravestone is taken as the starting point for your lichen growth. You can then measure your lichen and see how large it has grown in a given time period.

The best lichens to measure are crustose lichens which tend to have a roughly circular growth pattern and the most commonly used is Rhizocarpon geographicum which is a yellow/green/black speckled crustose lichen. Any lichen with a circular growth pattern will work. If you are calibrating in a local churchyard try to ensure that you find a lichen that grows in the graveyards and the wall you wish to age and you will be fine.

When measuring, try to find roughly circular growths of lichen and measure the radius of the growth from the centre point to the outer edge. Measure several lichens on several different graves to get an average growth rate for your

ancient hedge can accumulate species quicker than new hedges out on their own, this kind of new hedge may therefore appear older than it is. A final complication may be found in hedges further north than Derbyshire. Max Hooper's studies where carried out on southern hedges and the slower rates of growth in the cooler north can slow down the accumulation of species potentially giving a false indication of youth in a northern hedge.

area. You could even plot a graph of lichen age (based on the burial date on the gravestone) versus lichen diameter.

Once you get to your wall use this technique for measuring the same species of lichen and then read off the graph the age of the wall.

These techniques are obviously not entirely accurate as there are so many variables involved in the growth of the lichen including temperature variables, microclimate effects and substrate differences. You can minimise these variables by choosing a local church, a gravestone made of the same (probably local) stone and the same orientation as your wall. With these provisos you can gain a reasonably good estimate of the age of your wall.

Beware walls that have been built from rocks that already had lichen growing on them. Check a few colonies from various points along the wall to eliminate this problem.

If you don't have time to calibrate your lichen in a local churchyard you can use a rough estimate to calculate the age of the wall. Measure from the centre of the colony to the outer edge to get the radius of the lichen colony in centimetres. Multiply the radius by five to get the age of the wall. This will give you a rough estimate of the latest date that the wall could have been built.

# Notebook • The history of fields

There is a long history of fields and farming in this country with fields and boundaries being developed in each age, grubbed up and removed in the next and then reinstated in the following one. Some field systems are remakes of a previous one, whereas in other eras they created a whole new system of management and division.

The earliest field boundaries, still in existence, date back to the Bronze Age (2000 to 600 BC). In the Bronze Age there was a great dividing up of the land for arable and pasture, by long, straight boundary walls known as reaves, still visible in Dartmoor and County Mayo. In addition to the reaves there were Bronze Age field boundaries which were usually earth banks with large boulders at their core. The boulders were either so large they could not be moved and the field boundary diverted to take them in or they were smaller boulders cleared from the field. These boundary banks can still be seen in Cornwall.

Celtic and Iron Age field remains (c.400–20 BC) are typically smaller geometric fields which can be seen across large areas of downland and moorland that was not cultivated in later medieval times and so has retained these earlier structures.

The earliest records and remnants of hedges come from around Anglo-Saxon times after the Romans had left around 400 AD.

The biggest upheaval in field structures came in the Middle Ages as open field and strip cultivation techniques were employed across about a third of the country (Rackham 1994) removing many of the existing field structures and boundaries. The landowners divided their land into strips that their tenant farmers cultivated. One-tenth of the resulting

The open-field system was dismantled from the 1600s onwards and finally with the Enclosures Acts between 1845 and 1773 and it was now that hedges really took off. It is estimated that 200,000 miles of hedge were planted between 1750 and 1850, at least equal to all those planted in the 500 years previously. Over the years since then hedges have been replanted and moved periodically although in many areas the medieval patterns can still be seen.

The next most dramatic change to fields and hedges occurred between 1950 and 1975 when mechanisation and intensification in agriculture, particularly in the eastern counties, resulted in the great loss of hedges as fields were combined to accommodate the large tractors and harvesters. Hedges are now being replanted again as the benefits of the habitats provided by hedges, as well as the protection they provide in preventing soil loss, are finally being realised and hedge planting incentives are now available for farmers in lowland areas.

harvest was claimed by the landowner from his tenants. The small strips of land were ploughed year on year and resulted in 'ridge and furrow', wave like undulations that can still be seen across much of England from Oxfordshire to Edinburgh in pastureland that is no longer cultivated. This system had few hedges or walls but relied on paths or uncultivated strips of land to mark out the cultivated areas. There would have been hedges around meadows and pastures from this period. Remnants of the open field system can still be seen Haxey in Lincolnshire, Soham in Cambridgeshire, Portland in Dorset and Braunton in Devon (Rackham 1994).

Spotting migrating birds

*Easter, Greek Islands*

... I was on look out at the prow of the boat today, keeping my eyes peeled for dolphins and porpoises. I'm completely obsessed with the desire to see some marine mammals so I spent every moving moment scanning the water all around to ensure that we didn't miss a sighting. Sitting cross-legged on the deck peering crinkle-eyed as the sunlight spikes off the mini wavelets, I didn't spot a dolphin but I did spot a tiny dot. I kept my eyes on it and it slowly resolved itself into a tiny bird. It fluttered gamely across the surface of the water. We were completely out of sight of land and it looked so tiny and vulnerable out there all alone. It had clearly spotted the boat and took the chance of a rest, coming to perch on the mast just above my head. I imagined I could almost hear it puffing as settled down.

It's amazing to think that this tiny speck of life has probably come all the way from sub-Saharan Africa. While I'm aware this migration takes place each year, seeing this minute bird battling its way across this vast sea really brings home the mammoth investment these fist-sized birds put into making their way to their breeding grounds and a good supply of insects. Eventually this little one took off again and I wished it well, hardly believing that it can possibly make it through all the hazards and just the sheer distance that stands between where we were in Greece and the coast of England.

But who knows – it had made it this far ...

## How to watch migrating birds

Most migrating birds travel in flocks and fly much higher than the little bird I spotted. The flocks on the edge of the land make an impressive sight as they make landfall or set off on their journey.

The time to see migrating birds is in spring and autumn. When the seasons change, so too do the bird species that need to move to find more suitable weather or feeding conditions. In spring, birds that have been overwintering further south, possibly as far as southern Africa, follow the supply of insects north to breed in the rich summer feeding grounds in Britain. At the same time those birds that have been with us for our mild winter conditions, typically the wetlands birds and waders, find it gets too warm so they head north to the Arctic Circle where the short summer has rich feeding and good conditions for breeding.

The time to see migrating birds
is in spring and autumn. When
the seasons change, so too do
the bird species that need to
move to find more suitable
weather or feeding conditions.

Again, in autumn, the big change around takes place. It starts to cool down and insect numbers decline and it is time for the small-bodied insect eaters to head south to find warmer conditions and rich insect communities. Around this time the large bodied wetland birds are finding the Arctic is getting too cold and they fly in to enjoy our maritime winters and good feeding in the coastal muds and marshes.

### SPRING MIGRATION

Throughout April and May, depending on the weather conditions it is possible to see migrants arriving in large numbers from their winter-feeding grounds nearly 10,000km away in Africa.

All around the southern and eastern coast of England the southern migrators can be seen returning. The birds you can expect to see are swifts and swallows, House Martins, Spotted Flycatchers, cuckoos and nightjars in great numbers as well as Sand Martins, Blackcaps and Whitethroats. Waders such as the Dunlin, Turnstone and Godwit are also seen passing through the UK on their way to more northern, Arctic breeding grounds.

It is not only the small insect eaters that find their way to our shores in summer, the Hobby and some other birds of prey move in to eastern areas of the UK, from Europe, to make the most of the influx of small birds.

In addition to our anticipated summer visitors there are inevitably a few rarities that find their way to our shores. These are usually birds that have been blown off course or have overshot their usual European destinations. Typical overshoots may include bee-eaters, Hoopoes and Black Kites as well as non-native sandpipers. It is a busy time

## Finding southern migrators

**Coastal areas** along the south and east coast of England are all potential arrival and departure points for birds to and from the south.

**Spurn Head, Yorkshire:** up to 22,000 swallows and 7,000- house martins have been seen arriving on consecutive days.

**Alderney, Channel Isles:** many migrating birds

**Portland Bill, Dorset:** huge numbers of swallows and martins funnel down this finger of land out into the first stage of their intercontinental journey.

The southern sea cliffs of **Dover, Swanage and Purbeck (Dorset)** are all good viewing points as well as the east coast of East Anglia and right up in to Yorkshire.

for twitchers keen to add these one-off visitors to their list of species (table above).

### AUTUMN MIGRATION

In September or October, it is a common sight to see swallows and starlings lined up on telephone wires preparing themselves for the long journey, until one day all the practice gatherings become the real thing and they are off. Throughout the country these flocks are accumulating and heading south. The flocks build the further south in the country you go until huge numbers can be seen on the southernmost areas of land. Along the south coast of England flocks congregate in wave after wave of small birds waiting on telephone wires for ideal conditions to set off.

Huge mixed flocks of migratory species aggregate above reed beds where they roost for

## Finding winter flocks

**Hickling Broad, Norfolk:** raptors fly in to roost in large numbers October to March including Marsh Harriers, Hen Harriers, Merlin and owls.

**South Walney, Cumbria**

**Thurrock Thamesside, Essex**

**Gibraltar point, Lincolnshire:** wader flocks fly when they tide is high and they are forced off the ground. Plan your visit around a winter high tide for the best spectacle.

**Montrose Basin, in northeast Scotland:** huge numbers of Pink-footed Geese in November

**Pwllpatti, Radnorshire**

**Wheldrake Ings, Yorkshire**

**Blashford Lakes, Hampshire**

**Oare marshes, Kent**

**Cley Marshes, Norfolk**

**Isle of Muck, Ireland**

Particularly numerous are the geese: Greylag, Brent, Barnacle, Canada and Pink-footed and the ducks: Mallard, Pintail, Shoveler, Eider, Tufted, Shelduck, various swans and many other birds including Snipe and Woodcock, Knot, Lapwing, plovers, Dunlin, Redshank, Curlew and Shag. In addition to the wetland flocks many of the birds of prey move down from the high land to overwinter in the valleys and lowlands. This can be a great opportunity to see significant accumulations of birds of prey as they come in to roost.

### WHERE TO SEE WINTER FLOCKS

Large numbers of ducks, geese and waders accumulate in wetland and estuarine areas throughout the UK in the winter months. Some outstanding flocks can be seen at the places given in the table, left.

### MURMERATIONS

Another spectacular sight, not directly related to migration, are the huge flocks of starlings, known as murmerations, which gather in the winter months to roost. The peak time to see them is just before dusk in late November and early December but they can be seen right through to February. There can be anything from a thousand up to a million birds in these flocks, providing warmth and safety to the individuals.

These huge flocks produce one of the most stunning displays in the natural world as they fly. Their numbers build and build at sunset, with the flock twisting and turning to create smoke-like patterns in the sky before the birds finally settle down to roost.

While it is possible to chance upon these

the flight. House Martins don't join the reed bed roost preferring bridges and tree canopies. Typical launching points include Portland Bill on the south coast where the flocks funnel off the main landmass, launching themselves on their runway following the direction of this narrow finger of land.

Although we lose much of our small bird population in the winter months we also welcome winter visitors from the Arctic zone to our milder winters. These birds do not breed here but join our breeding populations and congregate in large numbers and feed on our estuaries and wetlands.

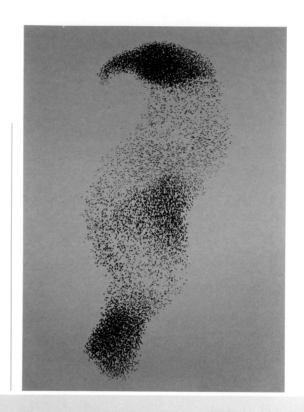

displays serendipitously there are some places that typically have excellent shows.

**WHERE TO WATCH MURMERATIONS**  Have a look at your Local Wildlife Trust website or RSPB reserves and find out where you can see murmerations near you. Some particularly good and accessible displays can be seen from the Brighton and Blackpool Piers, Gretna Green and the Somerset levels. The Somerset Wildlife Trust has a hotline providing details of where their local murmerations are happening which they keep updated in winter.

# Notebook ·
## Bird migration

Spotted Flycatcher

Travel is a human fascination and the amazing journeys that animals perform as part of their natural cycles are most intriguing and almost unbelievable. Early theories had birds sinking in to the mud on river beds over winter or even flying to the moon rather than taking a journey of 10,000km across oceans and continents and back again. The ringing of birds at the end of the 19th century finally proved the existence of migration and put paid to other fanciful theories.

In evolutionary terms long migrations are quite a new phenomenon; just 14,000 years ago northern Europe was under ice. However, as the ice retreated and seasonal variations in productivity spread across the newly available land animals began to move further and further to make the most of food resources. Migration allows animals to follow the food as the earth's rotation angles a different part of the planet towards the sun throughout the year.

## Adaptations for migration

– Migration is a risky business for a small bird and only the best prepared have any chance of survival. There are many physical and behavioural adaptations that have developed to give them the best chances of survival.

**Feeding and efficiency** To survive their long journey birds often need to bulk up. It has been shown that in some cases their internal organs – stomach, gut, liver and kidney – reduce in size during migration to allow their heart and lungs to increase for greater flight efficiency. Once they have reached their destination their internal organs return to their resting size to allow the birds to feed most effectively (Pioroma 1998). The efficiency of these birds as they travel over thousands of miles is astounding. Calculations have been done on the Blackpoll Warbler that estimate that they do the equivalent of 720,000 miles to the gallon – my car claims it does about 75mpg.

Swallows and many other insect feeders travel in small loose flocks of 30 to 50 birds in daytime which allows them to feed on the wing. Other birds travel at night to reduce the risks from predators which means they are not able to feed on the go and have to allow time for scheduled feeding stops.

Swifts

**Navigation** Swallows make their first migration before they are five months old. As soon as they fledge the nest at three weeks of age they are building up a picture of their home territory for when they return to breed after their first migration. Birds use a number of techniques for navigation on their long journeys. Migrating swans and geese learn their migratory routes from family members and so stick with their families in 'V' flight formation. Smaller birds travel in loose flocks along with whichever birds are around. The day-migrating birds use the position of the sun as well as their internal magnetic compass on the longer sections of their journey then, when they get close to known territory, they will use their visual knowledge of the topology of the area to locate themselves.

Night-flying birds use the stars and the rotation of the night sky about the fixed point of Polaris (the North Star) as their navigational cue, as well as magnetic fields.

All birds have acute low frequency hearing allowing them to hear wind patterns from kilometres away so they can anticipate the edge of landmasses as well as mountain ranges etc.

**Timing of migration** Migration starts at the same time for individuals of the same species. It appears that for many birds day length determines when birds set off on migration as well as hormones in the reproductive cycle. Hormonal controls are particularly important in the spring migration when they are returning to their breeding grounds, while day length seems to be more of a factor in the autumn migration.

**Other challenges** There are many challenges that the small birds face on migration. The Sahara Desert is a big challenge for swallows comprising 1500km of waterless, food-less heat. The swallows stop to rest and refuel before attempting the crossing. Night-flying birds have an advantage here as the cooler air prevents the overheating of their hardworking muscles.

Storms are a problem: swallows have pressure sensors in their middle ears that allow them to forecast bad weather and storms. They will either make detours or land to avoid storm hazards.

Predators are a constant risk. An estimated 5000 million migrants fly south across Europe every autumn, presenting a great source of food to predators. Some of the falcons time their breeding or migration to make the most of the travelling feast. The Hobby changes its food supply from insects to small birds at this time of year as it fattens up to withstand its own migration down to Africa.

People are also a risk to the birds. Mediterranean countries capture many migratory birds and in sub-Saharan Africa, where the birds accumulate in their millions after crossing the Sahara, the small birds are trapped for food. Swallows have 300° vision to help them spot predators.

Even with all these adaptations there are great losses on migration. In a flock of 30 birds only a few may survive the journey to their breeding grounds.

*At home, Autumn*

... I stepped out early this morning and, walking up the garden path, was struck by the almost complete coverage of the bushes in spangled chains of diamonds glinting in the early, low sunlight. The orb spiders are always busy but it is only on a morning such as this that their industry is in such dazzling evidence. Every string of their webs was strung with a line of dancing, kaleidoscope water droplet baubles. Catching the early morning light and inverting the reflections of the plants around them, they glinted and glistened with prisms of light. Never has the common spider's web been so beautiful ...

## How to look for spiders

Spiders are amazing and varied creatures which build the most beautiful webs. In the UK none are poisonous and they only do good things, by eating flying pests, so we should love them as Miss Spider points out in Roald Dahl's *James and the Giant Peach*. Spiders can be found living in virtually all habitats. Some love nooks and crannies in walls, some love woody plants and others love low grasses, some even love the space between the wing mirror and door frame on my car. The easiest way to spot a spider is by the evidence of their webs that come in a wide array of shapes and forms. Each species of spider will spin its own distinctive web and if you are able to identify the web you can identify the spider. Different web structures include:

The **orb web** which is the traditional spider web shape. It hangs vertically with a spiral design around a radiating axis of silks.

**Tangle webs** are messy looking and designed to catch unsuspecting prey.

**Sheet webs** are typically horizontal sheets of spun silk.

**Funnel webs** are shaped like funnels that narrow to a neck where the spider lurks ready to pounce if their prey steps on the wider skirt.

**Tubular webs** wrap around trees. These are made by bark spiders that live in sheltered forest areas.

**Dome** or **tent webs** have threads hanging down over a sheet web. The threads knock the prey down onto the sheets where they are trapped by the sticky threads.

Spiders can produce different kinds of silk for the different parts of their web. They have a sticky silk to trap their prey; a non-sticky thread that goes around the structure that they can walk on; a stiff silk, that nursery webs and egg sacs are spun from; and the long thin silk, known as balloons of silk, that spiders use to capture the wind and transport them to new locations.

Some countryside spiders can be found

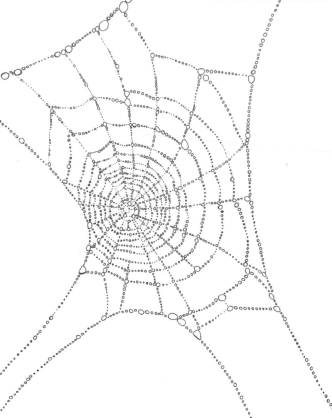

year-round but the vast majority are summer-only adults that cannot survive outdoors in the winter months. The best time to see spiders is in the summer and early autumn and particularly early in the morning when their webs often sport their water droplet decorations and become infinitely more visible and beautiful.

The orb webs that coated my garden with diamond necklaces on that autumn morning were probably spun by the common garden spider. In summer and autumn they spin their webs overnight ready for the next day. They have quite round bodies of around 1cm diameter for the males and 1.5cm for the females. They die off in the cold nights around November. These orb web spiders typically sit in their webs waiting for unsuspecting flies to get caught in its sticky threads.

# Notebook • Some interesting spiders

Funnel-web Spider

Walking along a field side path in Norfolk recently I was struck by some funnel shaped webs. Closer inspection revealed a cluster of young spiders on guard at the mouth of each of the tunnels. Just the slightest touch and they all dashed pell-mell into the depths of the web. These funnel webs are inhabited by the funnel web spiders often seen in rocky crevices and usually they are not accompanied by the young spiders at the entrance. Sometimes if you look down the funnel you can see the spider lurking ready to pounce on her unsuspecting prey. To entice her out you can just touch the collar of the funnel with a piece of grass and she will rush out ready to catch her supper.

A common British relative of the tarantula is the Wolf Spider. They are a fast running family that run around pouncing on their prey capturing many garden pests. They can often be seen on sunny days basking on open soil or leaves and fence posts.

Money spiders are tiny spiders less than 5mm long that spin sheet webs. They can often be seen at certain times of year as the early morning sun catches their threads ballooning behind them as they move on gentle air currents to new territories. They often get caught in hair and this was seen as good financial fortune. If you find a money spider you should spin it around your head by its thread three times before letting it go.

Nursery web spiders carry their eggs around in their jaws, a large ball dangling beneath them. Once the spiderlings hatch they build a kind of tent around them, often suspended between a collection of grass stems, they can look almost like some kind of cocoon.

The Four-spot Orb Weaver is another common orb web weaving spider frequently seen on grassland, heathland and common land throughout the UK. It is easily identified by its bulbous-shaped abdomen and has four distinctive white spots on its back. It weaves large orb webs of up to 40cm width, up to a height of 1.5m above ground. It weaves itself a silken retreat at the side of the web that it hides in ready to emerge and capture its prey.

Money spider

... Alexander Beetle appears in the poems of A A Milne. My mother introduced me to Alexander Beetle and on childhood walks we would always keep our eyes peeled for him. I would always find Alexander Beetles and I still do. I don't know if there is a definitive beetle that A A Milne had in mind but I have a selection that fit the bill. A black, active, shiny beetle with little beaded antenna, my Alexander Beetles are variously identifiable as some kind of ground beetle. I can't resist an Alexander Beetle when I see one and always have to bend down to have a good look and a chat. I see him everywhere. Regularly beetling across a soil path and even across the kitchen floor ...

## INTERESTING INSECTS

The countryside is full of beautiful and varied insect life and in this country the bonus is that very little of it is dangerous, although admittedly some can be slightly nibbly and irritating.

**GLOW WORMS**  On the walk home from the pub in the dark last summer as we descended the scarp of the North Downs we saw the glow of a glow worm. We went up close to have a look whist trying not to disturb this bioluminescent beetle. The North Downs is the only place I have seen glow worms in this country. The greatest glow comes from the female beetle trying to attract a mate, although the larvae and males do glow – just less brightly. Females have only a few weeks to attract a mate before they will die so they have to make their statement as brightly as possible. Peak glowing time is evenings in June and July and they are said to favour chalk grasslands but have been spotted throughout the country. Disused railway lines, grassy banks, verges and hedgerows seem to be prime sites for spotting them. They may be more common than you think. Just go out in the dark and don't use a torch – their light can not compete.

**GROUND NESTING WASPS AND BEES**  While out in areas with dry soil paths or exposed substrate banks you may often see a small, circular hole with substrate thrown up around it. This could well be the home of a ground nesting bee or wasp (digger wasp). These bees and wasps are solitary insects: the female builds a nest for her young rather than living in a colony as other bees, particularly honey-bees and wasps do. Some ground nesting bees and wasps will provide a food supply, lay their eggs and then seal up the nest. Others have stronger maternal instincts and will just provide a small food supply for the initial feed and then once the larvae have emerged they

will return to the nest and provide additional food. Although these bees and wasps are solitary there will often be several bee or wasp nests in one area where the conditions are suitable. Bare, dry ground in the vicinity of species-rich grassland is the place to look for these nests. It provides the ideal substrate for the nest while the species rich grassland provides nectar for food.

**GRASSHOPPERS** The striations of grasshoppers are the sound of the countryside on a warm and balmy day. There are 27 species of native grasshoppers and crickets but the most common grasshoppers are the Field and Meadow Grasshoppers and the Mottled Cricket. They make their song by rubbing their legs against their wings. The Field Grasshoppers like to hang out in sunny spots amongst short grass and can be found throughout the UK. The adults are typically seen in June and July although they will hang around as long as the warm weather lasts. In particularly mild autumns individuals have been found in December. The Meadow Grasshopper is found alongside the field grasshopper but is slightly larger, can't fly and

prefers longer grass. It is found throughout the British mainland but absent from Ireland. Mottled Crickets like very short vegetation and the hottest weather, they are also found throughout the UK in the summer months. They sing in the sunshine getting faster as the temperature increases so you can actually tell the temperature by the speed of their striations.

Alongside the grasshoppers there are also the groundhoppers, bush crickets and true crickets. The bush and true crickets sing (stridulate) by rubbing their forewings together and they usually sing at dusk or night.

**CUCKOO SPIT** Wherever there is grass or tall plants in late spring there is cuckoo spit. Looking exactly like spittle and appearing around the time of the first cuckoo call of spring, the clump of frothed up plant sap actually hides the nymphs of the froghopper bugs. Look inside the froth and you will see the small green nymph of the froghopper. The froghopper nymph feeds on the sap of the plant and produces the frothy spittle that hides the bug and has an acrid taste protecting it from predators. It also keeps the bug at a constant temperature and damp, stopping it from drying out. Eventually the froghopper emerges as a mature bug, brown coloured and possessed of a huge leap. Creating 400g of acceleration (humans can tolerate 9g before they pass out) it can leap further than a flea.

# Fossick for fossils

*Hunstanton, Norfolk*

... Heading off to the north Norfolk coast for a geology field trip with our schoolteacher was always a journey into the past. The journey itself, in his small MG, windows open to accommodate his pipe smoking, felt like a journey from a bygone age. Head back, pipe clenched between his teeth, luxuriant beard rustling in the wind, we would speed down the narrow lanes anticipating with excitement the day of discovery ahead. Once there we would unload our tools: geological hammers and chisels, field lenses, safety glasses, pens and notebooks; and of course packed lunch, and head down to the eroding cliffs to see what delights had been exposed in the most recent action of the sea.

The vivid colour change between the layers of orange Carstone sandstone, red Hunstanton limestone and white Ferriby chalk demonstrate perfectly sedimentation processes throughout the Cretaceous period (108 to 99 million years ago) and capture many unsuspecting creatures making great fossil hunting. On most visits we would find pieces or complete examples of ammonites, belemnites, bivalves, brachiopods and sponges; one of our major highlights was a shark's tooth. The best fossil rocks are the ones higher up the rock face – well beyond our reach – so we rely on the sea to erode big chunks out of the cliffs that are then conveniently lying around on the beach for us to investigate ...

## How to search for fossils

It is quite possible to go fossil hunting without specialist equipment but if you plan on breaking open some rocks you will need hammers and chisels and eye protection, plus a field lens to magnify your find.

There are different techniques to employ when looking for fossils depending on the type of rock you are looking in.

If you are searching for fossils in a slate area or fast eroding sea cliffs then you may not need a hammer at all. In slate areas, such as the Lake District, Wales and southwest England there are usually piles of ready broken slate in spoil heaps or scree slopes at the base of rocky outcrops. On fast eroding cliffs, typically on the east and south coast of England, there is usually a good supply of recently fallen rock to investigate, especially if you go down soon after a storm or extreme high tide before other fossil hunters have a chance. In these areas it is possible to sift through the fallen rock and on the exposed rock faces to see if any fossils have been exposed.

*TAKE CARE!*
*Don't try to climb the cliffs to get at the fossils, many cliff faces in the UK are extremely unstable or soft and will not be strong enough to take your weight.*

In many rock areas a hammer and chisel will greatly add to your fossil hunting experience. Once you have found a good location with some exposed rock to investigate you can get started. Pick yourself a good-sized boulder. Before you get going with your hammer examine the boulder carefully. You should be able to see layers or lines in the rock. These lines reveal which way the layers of sediment were laid down. You need to split the rock along these layers of sediment. Sedimentation happens very slowly so it is most likely that a fossil will be laid down in the same plane as the sediment. If you break your rock across the layering then you will almost certainly damage any fossils held within. If you break the rock along the lines then there is a slim chance that a fossil will be revealed.

Take the chisel end of your hammer, lay it along the line of your sedimentary rock boulder and give it a sharp tap. If it is soft enough and you have found the plane correctly it should break apart with nice flat edges. If not, give it a harder tap until it does. If you haven't managed to locate the layers correctly find another boulder and have another go.

If you are searching in chalk then the layers are hard to find and it is less productive to spend ages crunching rocks in the hopes of finding a fossil. For chalk rocks you are most likely to have success if you look closely over the surface of the exposed rock or boulder until you see something that may be the end of a fossil and then carefully excavate what you have found. Flints in chalk can look very like fossils and be very misleading; sometimes they even are fossils.

Don't be disappointed if it takes you a long time to find a fossil. If you think about all the events that have to fall into alignment for the boulder in your hand to contain a fossil then you will appreciate how lucky you will be to find anything.

*TAKE CARE!*
*If you plan to look at fossils on sea cliffs remember to check the tides before you go. Sea cliffs, by their very nature, generally have water right up against them at high tide, so check out tide tables and give yourselves a good amount of time to get to and from the cliffs either side of your hunting. Tide times can be found in paper tide tables usually sold at newsagents, post offices and shops near the coast. They will also often be posted up on notice boards near access points. Failing that there are good tide-table apps for your phone and several websites post them as well. The BBC weather website has short range tide tables for sites around the UK as well as the weather forecast.*

## WHERE TO FIND FOSSILS

Remember that only sedimentary rocks will contain fossil remains. As sedimentary rocks are present to some extent across most of the country that should not limit your hunting too much.

There are many good fossil hunting areas throughout the UK and they are not all at the coast. The trick is to find rocky outcrops of fossil bearing rocks. Good locations include sea cliffs, disused quarries where man has exposed the cliffs or mountainous areas where tectonic plate movements have pushed up the rock and weathering has exposed the face. The age of the rocks will determine which fossils you are most likely to find.

**THE OLDEST FOSSILS**  The very oldest sedimentary rocks are found in the far northwest of Scotland where a small sliver of ancient crust has reached the surface. Rocks this old hold fossils of the very earliest signs of life: minute fossils of bacteria and cyanobacteria (such as blue-green algae) going back 2,800 million years. As you travel south and east diagonally across the country there are bands of ever-younger rocks that have been laid down like blankets over the millienia. The rocks become progressively younger and the animals they hold will be increasingly developed in evolutionary terms.

**CAMBRIAN, ORDOVICIAN AND SILURIAN ROCKS**  There are four main bands of Cambrian, Ordovician and Silurian rocks, one in the far northwest of Scotland, one in the Borders, crossing from Stranraer to Berwick-upon-Tweed which extends into Northern Ireland, one forming much of the Lake District and one under the north and western half of Wales. The Cambrian rocks (542 million years old) are ancient shales, slates and sandstone, while the Ordovician (488 million years old) are shales and mudstones. Silurian shales and mudstone are 444 million years old. In the Cambrian rocks the earliest trilobites – prehistoric marine woodlice – can be found. It is the era of the beginnings of life. Skeletons

and shells first developed, so fossils became a possibility.

**FOSSILS OF THE DEVONIAN PERIOD**   The next diagonal band to be encountered to the south and east is the Devonian (416 million years old) with old red sandstone, shales, slate and conglomerates with some limestones. These rocks lie under Cornwall and Devon, South Wales and scattered areas in Scotland – John O'Groats and the Orkneys making the dramatic sea cliffs beloved of rock climbers: the classic sea stack of The Old Man of Hoy and the slabs of Baggy Point. Fossils include prehistoric fish including the armoured shark and giant arthropods: shrimps, lobsters and the next generation of trilobites. The largest arthropod was the length of a man.

**CARBONIFEROUS LIMESTONES, SANDSTONES AND SHALES**   On top of the old red sandstone in the southwest of England and Wales and in a strong band heading up from Nottingham and Stoke on Trent to Hadrian's Wall and on to the Firth of Forth are the carboniferous limestones, sandstones and shales (359 million years old). These are coal-bearing rocks and bear fossils from the era of giant ferns and trees; the rocks often display fronds and bark patterns as fossils.

**PERMIAN LIMESTONES, MARLS AND SANDSTONES**  Squeezed in between the Carboniferous and Triassic outcrops is a tiny strip of Permian limestones, marls and sandstones (299 million years old) reaching up just east of the line of the M1 from Nottingham up to Middlesborough. The end of the Permian marked the mass extinction and end of the dinosaurs that has exercised the minds of archaeologists for many years.

**TRIASSIC MARLS, SANDSTONES AND CONGLOMERATES**  Next to be crossed is the great big tick of Triassic marls, sandstones and conglomerates. The western Cheshire arm reaches from outcrops in Carlisle and the Solway Firth emerging again at Liverpool and Blackpool down to the River Severn Valley and back up the A1 to Middlesborough and the Tees Estuary. These rocks make the valleys of our midlands and therefore house our main roads and canals. They are rich agricultural land, having been cultivated for thousands of years. These rocks are not the best fossil hunting grounds.

**JURASSIC LIMESTONES AND CLAYS**  As you travel east you cross into the Jurassic limestones and clays. A Jurassic band crosses the country in a diagonal strip from Lyme Regis on the south coast up through Oxfordshire and the Cotswolds

and on up to the sea cliffs of Whitby and Filey. These rocks contain the classic fossils: whirled ammonites, cigar shaped belemnites and plesiosaurs (somewhere between a seal and porpoise).

**CRETACEOUS CHALK**  From the Jurassic you cross into a band of Cretaceous chalk. Forming an L-shaped band from north Norfolk down through Cambridgeshire down to the coast at Lulworth and across the south downs through Surrey and off through Kent forming the coastline between Deal and Worthing.

**TERTIARY CLAYS**  Overlying the cretaceous chalks, clays and sands are the Tertiary clays. These clays, the youngest rocks in this country, exist only in the far east of East Anglia, north Kent and London, with a small outcrop on the south coast under the New Forest and Poole and Christchurch harbours. The fossil remains here are animals that we can still relate to, laid down just 1.6million years ago – they will include mammals and marine animal remains.

There are good fossil hunting sites to visit in every county and region of the UK. Have a look at UKfossils.co.uk for a comprehensive list of sites to visit as well as lots of other resources about fossils.

Visit standing stones

*Castlerigg stone circle, Cumbria*

... We walked from Castlerigg stone circle today. It really is the most ridiculously picturesque stone circle imaginable. Not so much the stone circle itself but the setting. On a hillside up above Keswick, there are views down the Helvelyn range and out across Derwentwater over to Borrowdale. Today is particularly spectacular. Overnight it rained in the valleys but snowed on the tops, so every peak and ridge is iced with a frosting of snow. There are still rainclouds around and where they break the sun light shafts through, highlighting peaks and valleys like stars in a show. To cap it all a pair of nested rainbows broke through, spreading their magic. We have not had the best weather this week and there has been a lot of rain, however, it has mostly been broken cloud, so everyday we have been treated to this kind of light show. Every cloud has a silver lining – and some have rainbows too ...

## Standing stones

There are some 1300 stone circles in the UK and many of them are associated with other ancient monuments such as mounds, avenues and burial chambers. Stonehenge is probably the most famous of all the stone circles and is associated with a huge number of other structures in its vicinity but there are numerous other stone circles that are worthy of a visit too.

Stone henges date from the late Stone Age and in to the Bronze Age (around 3,300 BC to 900 BC) when farming communities started to erect these large stones in a circular formation within a circular ditch and bank.

No one really knows for sure what their purpose was, but they are often accompanied by numerous burial mounds, and often their orientation seems to be significant in terms of the sun or moon. Very often stones or entrances seem to have been erected to tie in with key days in the solar or lunar calendars. It seems most likely that they were ceremonial centres of some kind either for performing fertility rites, marking the cycles of life and death, feasting, worship or trading of goods. Some archaeologists maintain that any astronomical alignment or observed geology is purely coincidental.

Whatever the reason behind these henges, the communal effort required in building these structures would have been great and would have been immensely important in a community sense for the people and their families that were involved.

**WHERE TO FIND STANDING STONES**
The majority of the standing stones and stone circles that still exist lie in the west of the country. They are scattered from the far north in the Shetlands and Outer Hebrides, mainland Scotland throughout England and Wales and down to the very tip of Cornwall. The furthest

There are some 1500 stone circles in the UK and many of them are associated with other ancient monuments such as mounds, avenues and burial chambers.

east of all the stones circles is the Rollright Stones in Oxfordshire. Wood henges have been found further east – including the wood henge at Holme next the Sea and one in Arminghall both in Norfolk, so maybe the western dominance is just a feature of the materials available and less persistent wood henges were developed in eastern regions.

Most henges are built using locally found stone: the Rollright Stones originated within 500m of the site. However, Stonehenge is unusual in the distance some of the stones were transported for its construction. Sixty blue stones from the Preseli Mountains in Wales were transported to Stonehenge but further sarson stones came from Marlborough Downs much more locally. It did take around a century to develop Stonehenge so maybe that is why stone circles are rare anywhere further east!

Along with the ancient stone circles there are also many modern stone circles that have been erected much more recently for a variety of reasons. At Gatton Park in Surrey there is a stone circle that was erected to celebrate the millennium. Each stone represents 200 years and is inscribed by quotations or poems from that 200-year era. The reasons modern stone circle creators give for erecting their stone circles are variable and numerous. Many feel compelled to do it. Some erect them as modern monuments or memorials and some as intellectual investigations into methods and techniques – re-enactments.

If you would like to locate some stone circles to visit have a look at a map or search the net. Stone circles are marked on ordnance survey maps and there are also listings on stone-circles. org.uk which includes burial mounds and standing stones as well.

# Collect some antlers

... I was sorting out my large supply of postcards today and came across one I picked up at the Wildlife Photographer of the Year exhibition a few years ago. It was a beautiful picture of a Red Deer stag silhouetted by an orange sunset. Tangled in his majestic antlers is some vegetation, which makes him look as if he has several head scarves tied around his head. The juxtaposition of the aristocratic animal, head held high with a headdress on is wonderful – as though he's been caught half way through a dressing up game with his children ...

## How to find antlers

The Red Deer stag is very definitely the king of the British countryside. With his immense antlers he is forced into an upright, chest-out pose, as he struts around his domain.

One of the great pleasures in life is seeing our largest native mammal, the Red Deer, out in the wild. These majestic animals can be see throughout the country but are perhaps best seen out on the open hillsides of Exmoor or Scotland – the two main strongholds of the Red Deer's territory.

Every year the male Red Deer, the stag, grows new antlers. They break through in spring covered in their soft velvet skin. Rubbing their

**COLLECT SOME ANTLERS**

antlers against trees, rocks and posts the stags rub off the velvet in summer until the antlers stand proud and solid, glinting in the sunlight ready to attract a mate and fight off their rivals. The antlers are their main weapons in the autumn rut. This is when the stags protect their territory and their females against other stags. They will also do their best to encroach on other stags territory and females to increase their standing.

The size of their antlers is important as a statement of the stags' strength and virility. They

want to avoid a fight if possible, so they roar and strut and show off the size of their antlers hoping this will be sufficient to intimidate their rivals. Sometimes it does come down to a fight and then the antlers really are important as they can make the difference between winning and losing and even between life and death. Once the rut and the mating season are over for the year the antlers are no longer needed. The stag sheds them in winter, to save energy over the low food period, before re-growing them again in the spring. Each year that the antlers regrow they will be larger, by a prong, than the previous year until the antlers reach a maximum size. The size of the antlers therefore indicates the age and seniority of the stag.

The best time to look for cast antlers is therefore in winter and early spring. Antlers are prized by anyone who finds them and used for many crafts and items such as whistles, key rings and walking sticks so they don't hang around on the moors for long. The deer will often stay in the same places at this time of year and local antler hunters will often know the best places to go to find antlers. You may be lucky and come across one undiscovered in a remote spot at any time of year.

Antlers these days are used in decorative arts but historically they were invaluable as tools and weapons. In creating hand-held axes from flint a flint napper would usually use an antler hammer to chip the rock to the desired shape. In the digging out of ditches in the creation of henges, antler picks were used to channel out the chalk – these one pronged picks would have incorporated the shaft and lowest prong of the antler. Antlers were also used as ornaments and

adornments often being carved with intricate designs. At the Mesolithic archaeological site, Starr Carr in Yorkshire, 21 antler skull caps were excavated along with 200 harpoon tips – all fashioned from Red Deer antlers. They had been preserved in the waterlogged peat at the site and were an important find as usually the only surviving Mesolithic artefacts are flint tools.

Adventure is just on the right side of fear.
To be confident and in control in a situation where
things could get nasty, but aren't going to.

*Turnbull 2001*

# be
# adventurous

# Get off the beaten track

*Brecon Beacons, June*

... It is Dunc's birthday today and we set off *en famille* for an outdoor adventure. Dunc had spotted an idyllic hidden valley in the Brecon Beacons on a previous visit and wanted to show it to us. We set off along a clear track and headed up through heather on to the ridge. Before we reached the top of the ridge we began to descend. The shape of the mountain prevented us from seeing into the valley bottom and the descent was hard on our knees. We tried sliding on our bottoms but it was too tussocky and boggy for this to work. Eventually we reached the small stream that bounced around between the old red sandstone boulders at the base of the slope and headed down stream. Before long the trickle had gathered run-off water and was a more significant and determined flow. It meandered around in the limited space it had and suddenly spread itself out across the bottom of the valley in a delta of gravelly channels. Within ten metres they had all joined again into one channel, crossing a solid sheet of rock that suddenly plunged over a five-foot drop. At the edge the perfect sheet of water fell and dropped onto another stone ledge before crashing into a pool and continuing its journey. Running between mossy banks, winding between tree roots and rocks, with sheep nibbled banks on either side, it was beautiful and definitely required further investigation. We stripped off and swam and paddled and played in the waterfall before drying off and bundling up warm – mountain streams are never warm, even in summer ...

## How to get off the beaten track

Since the introduction of The Countryside and Rights of Way Act 2000 (CRoW) you legally have the right to roam on open access land. Check your maps carefully to make sure you are in open access land (the boundary is marked by a yellow line) and also check the terrain. If the area away from the paths is boggy – shown by little bunches of lines depicting tufts of bog rush – then it might be that the path is the best place to be. Otherwise why not try a new route and head out in to the unknown. You will need to be even more vigilant than you would be on the path and keep an eye out for changes in vegetation that could suggest bogs and hidden streams.

If you want a real challenge, set yourself a compass bearing and stick to it through thick and thin. This is the kind of training that explorers undertake to ready themselves for any situation

Try a new route and head out into the unknown. You will need to be even more vigilant than you would be on the path and keep an eye out for changes in vegetation that could suggest bogs and hidden streams.

that comes their way. The renowned Arctic explorer Pen Haddow lives on Dartmoor and trains this way – probably pulling an old tyre behind him as an extra challenge.

Once you get away from the marked paths you will find a whole new level of wilderness. We as a species are very set in our ways and find it hard to break out from the norm.

One of the joys of British wild places is that, even though we are a small, slightly overcrowded country, it takes very little effort to get away from the crowd. Think a little bit differently and or behave a little bit differently and you can have the countryside to yourself. Over the years we have observed that most people struggle to get out before 10am. If you need to get into a potentially busy car park arrive before ten and you will usually be fine. The same is true at the end of the day. With our national reliance on tea, there tends to be a mass exodus from the wilderness in time for a nice cup of tea, so you will find everything quietens down after five – even in the summer months. The same kinds of rules apply with distance. If you walk for more than an hour you are in to hardened walker territory and the numbers decline. Just getting away from the honeypot areas of popular walks can make a big difference in itself. Heading away from the path will also take you away from other people. Even on quite popular mountains you may find you have the day to yourself if you get off the beaten track.

*Great Gable, Lake District, August 1999*

... We set off late up Great Gable this evening weighed down by our bivvy bags and overnight supplies. I was doubly laden being seven months pregnant but at least I was balanced with the additional weight on my back. We took it slow and reached our camping spot beside the tarn, a sheltered nook between a couple of boulders but not obscuring the view across the tarn and down the valley. We had just enough light to get ourselves sorted out, brew up a hot drink and wriggle in to our bivvy bags, like a reversed film of a snake shedding its skin. We hadn't seen a soul on our way up the mountain and it was lovely to lie back on a bed of grass looking straight up as the stars dodging in and out of the scudding clouds. The next morning we awoke, slightly damp in the settled dew, but jumped around in our bags to shake of the surplus drops before shedding our 'skins'. As we had woken early so we had plenty of time to gather ourselves, have breakfast and climb the last few hundred metres to the summit of Great Gable. This time we were not alone. Several people had chosen this spot to experience the solar eclipse. It all went strangely quiet as the morning turned to dusk and night appeared to fall. The thin layer of cloud was such that we were able to watch the eclipse with our naked eyes through the veil of water droplets. A sheepdog huddled in close to his owners' legs, tail down, clearly not happy with what was going on. We all went quiet as it went dark and the sun's golden disc was slowly shut out. It was eerie and atmospheric but all returned to normal as the golden disc emerged again and we all relaxed, exchanged a few words and carried on with our walks ...

We took it slow and reached our camping spot beside the tarn, a sheltered nook between a couple of boulders but not obscuring the view across the tarn and down the valley.

## How to enjoy a bivouac

A bivouac is defined as any shelter that is less than a tent. A bivvy bag is pretty much just a waterproof bag to go around your sleeping bag. There are several bivvy bags on the market made by the outdoor manufacturers including RAB, North Face, Terra Nova, Kathmandu and so on. There is something particularly exciting about heading into the outdoors, travelling light with everything you need to eat and sleep for a couple of days, while still being able to walk upright and may be even run a bit. Without the usual camping paraphernalia, you can get in and out easily and unobtrusively. If you don't have a bivvy bag the next best thing is a lightweight tent.

Sleeping out in the open, under the stars, gets you close to nature in a way that is not an everyday experience in most of our lives. If it rains most bivvy bags have a hood you can zip close. The freedom of the bivvy bag can allow you to relax and take the day as it comes – a taste of

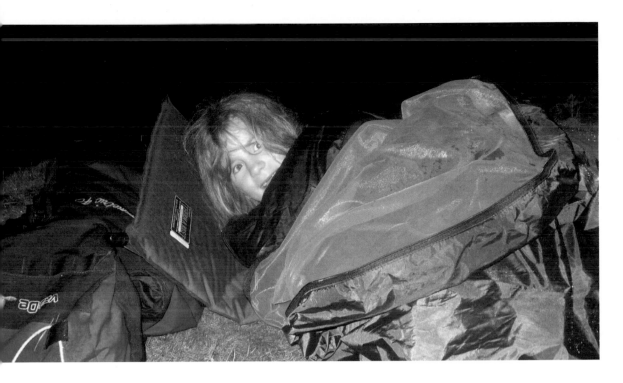

real freedom. You can stay out later and find some great remote spots to lie back and take in the view and often a great sunset.

Staying out overnight will guarantee you have the mountains and moors almost exclusively to yourself for several hours.

### HOW TO PLAN YOUR BIVVY

As with all things there is an art to making the most of a bivvy and maximising your comfort in the process. Follow these simple steps and you will be well on the way to a special adventure. Start to look for the perfect sleeping spot an hour before dark. Try out some spots for softness, shelter, view, privacy and slope.

The whole point of bivvying is to travel light. Take only what you need and nothing more. But I have a rule that you should always have one non-essential luxury. Some nice cheese, a glass of wine, a pack of cards or a dry pair of socks for bedtime.This is supposed to be fun so don't make it too much of a burden.

Don't get to your camp too early. There's only

so much fun you can have in a bivvy bag, so keep walking until it is bedtime and make the most of the day that way.

Live by the sun. Get up when the sun does, it will wake you up anyway and go to sleep when it goes down. That way you make the most of the day and the warmth.

The view is an important factor in bivvying. You miss half the point if you don't maximise the view. Up high is generally good, lakes, sea or rivers down below make the most of reflections. Do you want to see the sunset or the sunrise? Both is almost impossible, but one is a must.

Shelter is a difficult one as it almost always conflicts with the view requirements. Try to get away from the wind on the lee side of a slope or behind a copse or rocky outcrop. A small dip in the ground can be just enough that the wind passes overhead. If it is due to be a clear night then heat can be lost very quickly, it is surprising just how much difference some cover can make. A branch of a tree or a rocky overhang can make all the difference on a clear night.

The softness of your mattress and contact with the ground can make or break a bivvy. Pine needles, heather and deep grass are all very comfortable bedfellows. Anything that raises you off the soil will improve your warmth as well as comfort significantly. Being in direct contact with rock or soil is the quickest way to lose heat. If you know you will struggle to find anything comfortable to lie on it is worth taking a thin foam mat to lie on. Alternatively you could take your belongings out of your backpack and lie on that, but don't forget to take a waterproof bag for your belongings if you plan on using this trick.

Be warned that although moss promises much softness it only accumulates where it gets a good supply of water and often hides rocks, tree stumps or other hard substrates.

Don't forget your waterproof bivvy bag is quite slippery. If you are lying on short grass on a slope you will keep sliding away. Similarly if you use a foam mat and lie on that you will certainly keep slipping off. Put the foam mat inside the bivvy bag to avoid this problem as long as you are not on stony ground and risk damaging your bag. This is actually one of the hardest challenges in the mountains: I've had many ruined nights slipping and sliding around.

One of the main joys of being out in a bivvy bag is being away from civilisation. Make sure you are placed where you are not overlooking other people or where other people can see you. There is some pleasure in over looking a town or village lighting up at the end of the day but don't get so close that the lights keep you awake.

The law on wild camping varies from country to country. In Scotland wild camping is legal on open access land. In England and Wales wild camping is illegal without prior permission from the landowner. You may find that landowners will allow you to camp for a few days in an empty field but you must ask permission. Dartmoor National Park has its own amendment to the standard National Park legislation; wild camping is allowed as long as campers are discreet and responsible – wild camping is in fact tolerated in most wild places in the UK on this basis.

The Scottish Natural Heritage has put out this advice which should keep you on the right side of the law:

## Rules for wild camping

Wild camping should be lightweight, done in small numbers and only for two or three nights in any one place. Don't camp in enclosed fields of crops or farm animals.

Keep well away from buildings, roads or historic structures. If you wish to camp close to a house or building, seek the owner's permission.

Avoid disturbing deer stalking or grouse shooting.

Avoid overcrowding by moving to another location.

Carry a trowel to bury human waste and urinate well away from open water, rivers and burns.

Use a stove or leave no trace of any camp fire. Never cut down or damage trees.

Take away your rubbish and consider picking up other litter as well.

If in doubt, ask the landowner. Following their advice may help you find a better camping spot.

Access rights are not an excuse for anti-social or illegal behaviour.

## Hempnall, Norfolk, April

... Today we have borrowed a GPS from South Norfolk District Council. It is part of a geocaching 'give-it-a-go' scheme. They have set out some geocache points around the district and you can go into their offices to pick up information with grid references and clues, you can borrow a GPS if you don't have one and then you are on your own. So far it is not going well. We've been to the Roman archaeological site at Caister and while I was pretty confident we were in the right place we couldn't find the cache. We had a lovely time though; it is a fascinating site – probably an ancient Roman market place. Now we are trying Smock Mill Common. We used to come here regularly as kids when dog walking and sledging in winter, I even came here on an infant school trip, I think we came to look at the wildflowers and natural history but my main memory is of getting out of the minibus and coming face to face with an enormous dog that tried to lick my face and then lean on me. I always thought of it as being the size of a cow but since I was only five years old it was probably just a pointer or similar sized dog. We are not having much success with the geocache here and spend some time circling the common, it's lovely we are getting right in to the nooks and crannies and having a wonderful time exploring. When, eventually, we take it back to the start we realise we have been using the GPS on the wrong setting and find the geocache in minutes – success! But it has certainly kept us entertained and we have seen every square centimetre of the sites ...

## Navigation challenges

### GEOCACHING

Geocaching has become a world-wide treasure hunt phenomenon with around 2.5 million caches worldwide. There are innumerable geocaching locations throughout the UK and the website geocaching.com has all the information you need to get you started. The essence of geocaching is that you register for a free membership on line, enter your postcode and find a list of geocaches in your area. You then chose one to find, enter the coordinates in your GPS device and head off. The coordinates should take you to where the geocache is hidden and then you just have to find it – sometimes they are very well hidden and occasionally they have been removed! Once you find the geocache you open it, sign the logbook and then put it back where you found it. You can then share your geocaching experiences online if

you wish. All you need to get started are a GPS device, which could simply be a GPS enabled mobile phone and your geocache.com membership.

## LETTERBOXING

In a similar vein to geocaching but slightly more informal is letterboxing. This is when someone decides to plant a container in a natural feature and invite others to search it out. This is particularly popular on the tors of Dartmoor where it first started in the 19th century. We have spent many happy hours clambering under, over and around the granite tors searching out plastic boxes. Inside the box is usually some kind of notebook that finders sign and leave messages in for the next finders to read. There is also often a rubber stamp which you can stamp on you own piece of paper or notebook to keep a record of the places you have been. Some keen letterboxers have their own rubber stamp to 'sign' the books. It's great fun reading people's entries and then often following the same people around the tors and seeing their trail of messages as you find letterboxes on the way. There is even a website for the Dartmoor letterboxing community with a catalogue of all the letterboxes left on Dartmoor. The catalogue contains clues and grid references for each of the boxes so you can test your navigational skills. Once you have proof that you

countryside there are urban orienteering events as well. If you get hold of your local orienteering group you will find there are many events you can join in around your area. You will need to take along you own compass but other than that you will be given a map at the start of the event and be on your way. Each event incorporates colour-coded routes that are graded on the basis of their difficulty. There are events for every member of the family and even string events for very tiny children that just require them to follow the route of the string around a trail. Once you have some idea of what orienteering is all about you will find that there are permanent orienteering courses in some places. These are permanent posts marked with the orange and white square for which you can get hold of maps from your local orienteering club and then visit whenever you feel the urge. There are several near where we live and it is a fun way to spend the day with kids and a great focus rather than just a walk. If you are interested find out about your local club from the British Orienteering Society website.

have visited 100 letterboxes you can become a member of the Dartmoor Letterbox 100 club. Other letterbox locations include the New Forest and the North York Moors. Keep your eyes peeled and if you see a picnic box don't assume it is someone's leftovers – it may be there for a reason.

## ORIENTEERING

Orienteering is a more organised sport that incorporates fitness with navigational skills and is practised widely throughout the UK. The aim in orienteering is to follow a map and navigate your way around a series of checkpoints marked by a diagonally divided orange and white square. Although events typically take place in the

## Reigate, Surrey

... A chat with the neighbours always puts me in a good frame of mind and I regularly return from my morning school and shopping run with sore fingers from my shopping bags as I've been chatting too long. This morning I was talking to John Spencer about his printing presses. He showed me some test prints that he has been experimenting with, on the theme of pilgrims. They are beautiful, poster sized prints of a barefoot, staff holding monk making his weary way along the path of the Pilgrims' Way. The original inspiration for the artwork was the route of the Santiago de Compostella pilgrim route across France and Spain, however, it works equally well for the Pilgrim's Way that we live near in Reigate.

Our Pilgrim's Way is reputed to be the route of early pilgrims who made their way along the North Downs to Thomas Becket's shrine in Canterbury from Winchester. Actually, as with many good stories, there may be an even better one behind these alleged facts. It seems that the Pilgrim's Way is a recent name coined by an Ordnance Survey mapmaker in 1871. Historians now suggest that although some pilgrims would have used our route it is unlikely that they did so in vast numbers. In fact, the route known as Pilgrim's Way, is a much more ancient trackway which archaeological finds date back to 500 BC but may well have been around since the Stone Age. The ancient route extended from the narrowest point of the channel all the way to the religious complexes of Stonehenge and Avebury. It follows the southern slope of the North Downs, above the level of cultivated land and below the exposed flinty routes at the top of the downs. Archaeological evidence suggests it was also an important route in Roman times. This ancient route runs all the way to the coast at Folkestone so the Christian pilgrims would have had to branch north to get to Canterbury ...

The route known as Pilgrim's Way is an ancient trackway which archaeological finds date back to 500 BC but may well have been around since the Stone Age.

## How to find long distance footpaths

We have a long and extensive history in this country and there are many ancient drove ways and historical paths that can be walked, run and cycled. The historical interest of these paths adds to the interest of the routes that are very often set in beautiful countryside. The ancient nature of these byways and highways very often means you are in undisturbed country with all the richness and diversity that brings to the associated wildlife.

There are short and long routes throughout the country and a small amount of research should reveal many choices for an adventure of your own. Ordnance Survey maps mark long distance paths as a dotted green line with green diamonds along its length. They are easily spotted wending their way across most maps.

The Long Distance Walkers' Association website has a searchable database of over 1,300 UK paths which is another great starting point.

Fifteen long distance paths in the UK are designated as National Trails and administered by Natural England and The Countryside Council for Wales. These are all particularly well-established Trails and include such national treasures as Peddar's Way, Hadrian's Wall and Offa's Dyke Path. Several of these routes are much more than a day walk and there is plenty of advice on where you can stay on the route. The Scottish equivalents are the Long Distance Routes administered by Scottish Natural Heritage.

For a shorter challenge, search out one of the UK's ancient roads, tracks or greenways. We have an incomparable network of routes criss-crossing the country that are suitable for walking and running, riding and cycling. Many reach from town centres right out into the countryside.

Ancient droveways were routes followed when driving livestock to market – often all the way to London or from summer to winter pasture. They often date back to medieval times. Because of the need to accommodate livestock they are often wider than other footpaths and many have been converted into our current network of roads. Drove roads that can still be walked include The Ridgeway over the Berkshire Downs, and ridgeways between Shaftesbury and Blandford to Salisbury. Much common land was once used as grazing for livestock on the long journey to market. Droving ceased in the 19th century as agriculture changed and the railways took over.

As well as ancient droveways and footways there are many paths now that make the most of canals, old railways, forest roads and farm tracks. These are often great cycle routes.

# 170    Get up high

## Blencathra, Lake District, July

... It is definitely a day to get up high. There is virtually no cloud and very little wind as well. I have wanted to go up Blencathra for years but have been thwarted at every opportunity. Today it was finally my time.

We set off early, scrambling up the shiny, much climbed route on a sharp edge. We were following a young couple with a small dog that needed to be carried or lifted over whole sections of rock. The scrambling was fun. I love to move fast over rock: that balance of adrenaline but not so much that you feel the need to be roped on. As we looked down to our left we were directly above Scales Tarn, a vast reflective eye staring up at the sky. Once we had achieved the edge we sat at the top of the ridge to eat our lunch. As we sat, in the stillness I could hear the twittering of a Skylark. It appeared to be below me and as I listened it came closer until I was able to pick out, from the brown and green mottled background below me, the tiny shape of a Skylark ascending. It was a strange inverted experience to sit and watch a Skylark coming up until it was at eye level before it then parachuted back down to the ground around the tarn – the lark descending. That was a first for me, it is not unusual to hear the Skylark up above with the sky as background and lose the tiny speck at the height of its ascent but to be sitting waiting for it as it worked its way up seemed somehow cruel, I felt I was playing a trick on it ...

### HOW TO GET UP HIGH

To get up high is to feel on top of the world. Even with quite small children it can be possible to get up high. In fact I remember being amazed when our kids were just three and four and we set of on a short walk and found ourselves heading up the side of Catbells – the direct route. Not on any path, just up. Children enjoy a challenge and a target. It is very often better to have the challenge of going up one steep peak and reaching the top, which is tangible and understandable to the small mind, than a longer, flat, circular walk which apparently has no rhyme nor reason.

If you want to get up high then the best places to be in the UK are the National Parks. Dartmoor, Exmoor, Yorkshire Dales, Peak District, Brecon Beacons, Snowdonia, Lake District, Cairngorms and Trossachs as well as the Scottish islands are all places you can get up really high. There are also lesser hills and raises that will provide a good view and feeling of being on top of the world even in the relative flatlands of the east and south of the country.

To get up high is to feel on top of the world. Even with quite small children it can be possible to get up high; children enjoy a challenge and a target.

If you are inspired by lists or challenges then there are various mountain lists to tick off. In Scotland you can go Munro bagging. A Munro is any mountain in Scotland over 3000m high. The Scottish Mountaineering Council recognises 282 Munros with a further 227 subsidiary tops (tops over 3000m but not recognised as a separate mountain). If you whip those off a bit quickly then you could move on to the Corbetts at 2,500 to 3000ft and even the Grahams at 2,000 to 2,500m. Although these mountains are not high, walking and bagging hills and mountains in Scotland is much more dangerous than you would expect because of the Arctic and Atlantic mix of weather they enjoy. Thick fog and snowstorms have been the downfall, literally, of many experienced walkers in the rugged terrain of the Scottish mountains.

Not to be outdone by the Scottish, in the Lake District a challenge has developed to climb all 214 fells mentioned in Wainright's seven book series of *Pictorial Guides to the Lakeland Fells*. Walkers now bag Wainrights and the Long Distance Walker's Association keep a register of all those who have completed the full challenge.

Scrambling is my preferred technique of getting up high in the UK. Taking the shortest non-technical route up rock and river is physically challenging without needing to resort to ropes and safety equipment that slow down progress quite considerably. You will need hands and feet for scrambling but not ropes. There are

## Some classic routes...

Tryfan North Ridge, Snowdonia

Snowdon Horseshoe, Snowdonia

Striding Edge, Helvelyn, Lake District

Sharp Edge, Blencathra, Lake District

Cuillin Ridge, Isle of Skye

An Teallach, Northwest Highlands of Scotland

guidebooks that will guide you up scrambles in the Lake District, Peak District, Wales and Scotland but you will need to have some experience of moving over rock and many routes will not suit children. Make sure you are confident in your own and your companions' abilities before you head off up a scramble. A series of classic routes are given in the box, left. These are all big dramatic well-known scrambles but much smaller lower ones can also provide great fun and adventure.

# Notebook • Skylarks

An exultation is the collective noun for Skylarks but I have to say even a solitary lark can be quite exultant.

Although the Skylark is known for its ascension, drawn upwards into the sky until it becomes vanishingly small, the Skylark is in fact a bird that lives on the ground. They feed on seeds and insects and nest on the ground. The singing flight way up in the sky is the male showing off to his mate in spring: 'Look I can fly and I can sing and I can defy predators by being so brave so I am worthy of being your mate.'

There is something uplifting and heart filling about the dramatic flight and endless song of the Skylark that touches all of us and was immortalised in the poems of George Meredith 'Lark ascending' and Percy Bysshe Shelley 'To A Skylark' and the music of Vaughan Williams. To see such a small bird taking on the world cannot fail to give anyone a lift. The song is complex and varied and a sure sign that spring is sprung. When not exulting and ascending the Skylark is inconspicuous and easily missed. Somewhere between Sparrow and Blackbird-sized the Skylark is light brown with white sides to its tail and a short crest which can give it a rather ruffled look of surprise, rather like a teenage boy who unexpectedly and unaccountably finds himself out of bed before midday. Skylarks can be found in the open countryside year-round throughout the UK, anywhere from farmland to moorland. Their major display of singing is usually in evidence in spring as they prepare to breed around April time. Skylarks will aim for two to three broods a

season but nesting on the ground in mid-length vegetation this is often scuppered in cultivated areas by the mowing of grass and the harvesting of cereals. The inability to complete as many broods as they would wish has been given as the reason for their recent decline in numbers.

Because of the ascending element of their flight the Skylark has a place in mythology representing daybreak. The birds were also used as symbols of Christ by Renaissance painters, once again in reference to their ascending flight.

# Take off your shoes

*Reigate, Surrey*

... Duncan has been inspired by the barefoot running revolution. He's been reading *Born to Run*, an inspirational book about the Tarahumara, Mexican indians, to whom running ultra-distances, in bare feet, is a way of life. The book advocates barefoot running to improve your foot strength and gait. So Dunc decided to give it a go. He set off towards the park to have a run on the soft grass but his first error was heading down there in bare feet. He barely made it across the road before he stood on some broken glass and hobbled home leaving a trail of blood behind him. He didn't need stitches but with a lacerated toe it will be a few days before he can run with or without shoes. It was not an auspicious start to his barefoot running career ...

## How to go barefoot

Even though Dunc's first attempt at barefoot running was not an unparalleled success there is much to say for running without. I would not run barefoot on the roads. I believe that our bodies and natural shock absorption were designed for softer surfaces than tarmac. Road running is pretty bad for your body at the best of times so without some extra cushioning it seems like a really bad idea. I do, however, advocate taking your shoes off wherever you can. If your feet are anything like mine they are used to being in shoes and will be very soft and sensitive to the slightest nobble, bobble and spike so walking or running any kind of distance barefoot is going to be a challenge. That does not stop you from having barefoot adventures though. I love taking my shoes off whenever I get to a stream that needs fording and then just delay putting my shoes on again for as long as I can get away with it. When we were trekking in Madagascar, our Malagasy guide was exasperated by our boots and shoes. He was wearing flipflops or bare feet depending on his mood. There were no bridges and quite regularly we would need to ford a stream, he would just walk straight into it, out the other side and keep walking. We would stop, take of our shoes, wade through, stop, dry our feet, put our shoes back on while he muttered and tapped his foot. Quite often he would offer to carry us over the water just to avoid the delays.

Moss, sand, mud, clay, grass. They all feel great under your feet. You can bend over and feel the textures with your hands but nothing is quite the same as taking your shoes off and wriggling your toes around to feel the sensations of the substrate squeezing between your toes and around your ankles. Land crossed in bare feet leaves you with a completely different set of memories from a place. There are things going on in the ground that shoe wearers are completely unaware of. As with temperature variations in a river when you are wild swimming the soils heat and cool variably. Walk across a soil path on a sunny day, cross into a wood and over grassland

I love taking my shoes off whenever I get to a stream that needs fording and then just delay putting my shoes on again for as long as I can get away with it.

and the temperature varies as much as the texture. Touch gives us all an insight and forms a bond between those who are in contact. Research has shown that the most damaging thing to a young baby is never to be touched; children in orphanages deprived of human touch can be damaged for life. Touching the earth and being in direct contact with the ground brings an understanding and mutual exchange that cannot be created in any other way.

Not all terrain is good for going barefoot. Pick your moments well. A tamped down soil can often be the least demanding on the foot;

grassland can often hide tiny thistles and gorse and be much spikier than you had ever imagined while ploughed soil can harden to rock and be unbearable.

If you like the idea of going barefoot more frequently you can build up to it. Your feet will harden up the more you go barefoot. I used to go barefoot all the time when I was younger and had no problem with gravel paths. In Nepal while we were trekking everywhere wearing our heavy boots the Nepalis were walking for hours carrying heavy loads on mountain trails in their leathery, bare feet.

# Go on an Arthurian quest

**King Arthur is perhaps the leading legendary character of British history. There are so many stories and pseudo-historical facts that it is very hard to unravel his story. Is he just a myth or did he really exist? Or is it just a good story made better?**

Historians have long debated this fact and can't make up their minds so I probably can't unravel the problem for you either. There are lots of places around the country that claim some involvement in the King Arthur legends so why not go on a quest to investigate some of the beautiful places that he 'may' have been?

King Arthur is mentioned in a 9th century history book *Historia Brittonum* as a leader of post-Roman Britain but these texts are not necessarily reliable. The more consistent elements of the legend suggest that King Arthur was a great warrior king, the son of Uther Pendragon and Igraine of Cornwall, whose court was at Camelot. He was married to Guinevere. King Arthur oversaw a chivalric order of 12 knights known as the Knights of the Round Table. The knights fought for the King and went on many dangerous quests. One of those Knights – Sir Lancelot – betrayed King Arthur with Queen Guinevere. Arthur was fatally wounded while fighting Mordred at the battle of Camlann and was taken to the Isle of Avalon where he is said to be sleeping in a cave with all his Knights until he is called upon again to lead his people.

These bare bones of the story appear quite reasonable and believable, however, there are many embellishments and other more imaginative elements that have been added to pad out the legend and make some great stories

The slightly more fanciful aspects that have been portrayed in some of the classic tales of King Arthur include Arthur being brought up as a servant and educated by Merlin the wizard who lived his life in reverse. Arthur came to the throne because he managed to pull a sword out of a stone in a feat that no one else had managed. Mordred was variously seen his son, from his inadvertently incestuous relationship with his half-sister Morgause, his nephew, one of his Knights or possibly Guinevere's son. These details are all later embellishments that have all been added to make a great story.

The truth or otherwise behind the legend was further confused by the Tudor kings who had used their link to Arthur as the proof of their legitimacy to the throne. This resulted in the legend being vigorously defended during the Tudor era to protect the royal family. Modern historians tend to believe there was a person behind the legend but probably not a king with a band of knights as portrayed in the legends. Some scholars still insist that there may not be any real character at the base of the legends at all.

## WHERE TO LOOK FOR ARTHUR

There are many places in the UK that lay claim to links with King Arthur and where you can go and immerse yourself in the unravelling of this great story.

Possible contenders for the Isle of Avalon where Arthur and his knights are said to be resting include Bardsey Island off the Lleyn Peninsular in Gwynedd, the Eildon Hills near Melrose in Scotland and Glastonbury in Somerset. The monks at Glastonbury Abbey claimed to have dug up an enormous coffin with

an inscription that said it was the bones of King Arthur and Guinevere with a possible third set of bones belonging to Mordred. In 1278 there was a reburial of the bones in a tomb in front of the altar that was attended by Edward I. It is now believed this was just a publicity stunt for Edward I and the monks and there were in fact no bones at all.

There are several contenders for the location of Camelot, King Arthur's court. Cadbury Castle, near Glastonbury, is an ancient hill fort and claims that the ghosts of King Arthur and his Knights can be seen and heard riding out of the castle on the full moon and the summer solstice. Caerleon has a strong position in Arthurian legend as the real Camelot. There is a stretch of grassland known as King Arthur's Round Table

and others believe the cave in which he is sleeping is in Caerleon as well – so maybe it is Avalon and Camelot all in one? Tintagel, high on the north Cornish coast is also associated with the Arthurian legend.

Eamont Bridge in Cumbria has a circular earthworks bearing the name of King Arthur's Round Table and in Winchester Great Hall there is an elaborate medieval table known as King Arthur's Round Table – this is cheerfully acknowledged as a fake.

There are many great fictional representations of the life of King Arthur where you can immerse yourself in his legends – two particularly great versions are *Morte D'Arthur* by Thomas Mallory and *The Once and Future King* by T H White.

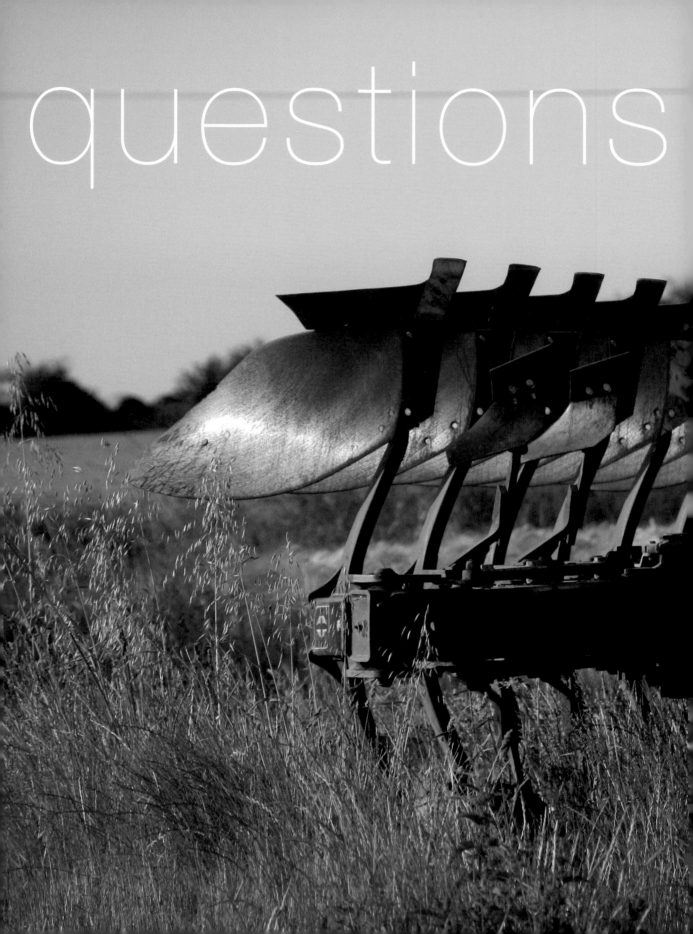

questions

What rock am I standing on?

**The geological map of Britain reveals quite a complex, blotchy situation with regards to the distribution of rocks across the country. A bit like the weather, there is quite a lot going on.**

On first look the situation is rather overwhelming and confusing but a deeper investigation reveals a slightly more understandable progression. If the rocks were colour coded based on their age, with the oldest being one end of the colour spectrum and the youngest being the other end of the spectrum then you would see a nice rainbow spread across the country. In general there is a progression in the age of the bedrock in a diagonal line across the country with the oldest being seen in the northwest of Scotland and northwest Wales and the youngest in the southeast of England.

One of the best ways to think about geology is to think of the rocks as layers or blankets laid down over time (Fortey 2010). Where they lie undisturbed the youngest rocks will be the ones nearest the surface. In some areas though, there will be disturbance. Volcanic activity and plate movements have tilted and churned and even pierced the blankets pushing some older rocks back up towards the surface. The modifying effects of weathering and erosion at the surface can also expose older rocks and bring them back to the surface.

The really fascinating aspect of geology for me is that most of our underlying rock is hidden from us but affects our everyday life. All aspects of the countryside from the wild flowers that grow there, the crops that predominate, the industry we practice, the nature of the houses and field

walls are all dictated by the rocks beneath our feet. If we just have a look around us we can use these clues to work out the type of rock we are standing on.

### FARMING

First look at the type of farming in your area. Farmers may decide to battle against the geology and farm subsidies will confuse the pressures on farmers but ultimately they will succeed more easily if they stick with what the geology dictates. If you are in an arable dominated area then your bedrock is probably sedimentary. This is true of much of England. But what crops are most common? Sandy soils favour carrots, while chalky ones suit barley and clay vales have the most deep and rich soils. In areas of resistant rocks where weathering is slow you get the upland areas where crops are rarely sown and the main animals farmed are hardy sheep.

The field boundaries are a real give away for the local geology. Where surface rock is readily available, field boundaries are mainly stone walls, in particular dry stone walls and the local geology is immediately revealed. Hedge boundaries predominate in soft rock and lowland areas and tell us only that there is a lack of available rock for wall building. In these instances, look to the buildings to gain more clues.

## BUILDING MATERIALS

Have a look at the local architecture, particularly the older buildings and churches. Flint buildings predominate in chalk areas, as do oak framed buildings inlaid with wattle and daub; the local stone is prevalent in harder rock areas and can colour whole villages, for example the butter yellow Jurassic limestone in Cotswold villages and the dark grey slate of Cumbria.

Roofing materials are dictated by the presence or lack of suitable roofing materials. Slate roof tiles predominate in north western areas, the southwest and Wales, while reed thatch roofing is common in south and eastern England. In the far east of Norfolk and Suffolk pan tiles imported from Holland became popular and can still be seen adding another flavour and information about historical links to the local architecture.

**LOOK AT COLOUR AND TEXTURE** Once you look more closely at buildings in the countryside the subtleties of stone colour and texture will allow you to locate yourself to within just a few miles. Even apparently quite standard brick properties will vary in colour relevant to the local materials used in their production. In my native Norfolk flint is the predominant rock used in old buildings but as well as the chalk bedrock that harbours the flints there are bands of clays that are turned into bricks. Many buildings combine the chalk sourced flint with clay sourced bricks – these bricks change colour with the various clay beds, so that those in the east of Norfolk are quite red while to the west they are paler and often with flecks of flint incorporated. Flints do not always signify chalk as the bedrock. Chalk being very soft and water-soluble erodes readily, while the much harder flint does not. Therefore flint can survive in areas where the chalk bedrock had completely eroded and an older rock is now in evidence in other outcrops. Beware of misreading such geologies.

## INDUSTRY

Evidence of a former coal mining industry suggests that you are on coal bearing Carboniferous rocks. These form a band starting in the southwest of England and Wales and heading up from Nottingham and Stoke on Trent to Hadrian's Wall and on to the Firth of Forth.

If you are surrounded by peat diggings in a highland area you may also see metamorphic rock outcrops. Ancient metamorphic rock can only reach the surface where volcanic activity has pierced the more recent blankets of rock or activity resulted in tight folds where the younger blankets have been rubbed away by weathering.

A land pock marked with spoil heaps and old mine workings indicates where minerals have been mined from igneous outcrops that reach the surface in particular in the North and far West of the country.

It is a great feeling to be able to look at our landscape and interpret something of our geology from some superficial characteristics. One of the beauties of the British countryside is that travelling around you can tell exactly where you are by the nature of the field boundaries, the plants in the hedgerows, the type of farming that is going on and the materials used in field boundaries, churches and old village buildings. These features change so rapidly you can locate yourself to within a few miles just by simple observation.

I carry a lot of guilt when it comes to Red Squirrels. I actually own a real, stuffed Red Squirrel that I inherited from an old family friend. Owning a stuffed version of an endangered animal in itself seems quite wrong. I have no idea how the poor squirrel met its end but even if it was a happy life with a natural end, it somehow doesn't seem right. This item also brings me guilt because apparently it was not intended for me. I don't remember this; I was very young at the time. Apparently the aged family friend was actually intending to give the stuffed squirrel to my brother Christopher who had an interest in taxidermy at the time. I seem to remember we had various bits of road kill in the freezer waiting for his skills to catch up with his interest. The story goes that I took a liking to Squirrel Nutkin in his glass fronted case and held on to it tightly until my brother eventually gave up on his claim – shame on me.

Once the only squirrel found in the UK the Red Squirrel population took a battering after the introduction of the Eastern Grey or American Squirrel. The Grey Squirrel can live at much greater densities that the Red Squirrel by feeding more efficiently in broadleaved woodland. The Red Squirrel has also fallen prey to disease – squirrel pox virus and road traffic. Red Squirrels are gradually being squeezed out by the Grey

Squirrels. There are currently reported to be 140,000 Red Squirrels but over 2.5 million greys.

There are still some Red Squirrel strongholds throughout the country where you can have a good chance of seeing reds. Brownsea Island in Poole harbour has no Grey Squirrels so the 200 or so reds are able to live in safety. The Island is owned by the National Trust and the only accommodation is a camping ground owned by the scouts and the castle owned by John Lewis so there are limited opportunities to stay there but you can catch a ferry out from Portsmouth and visit for the day. It is a beautiful place to visit with walking and orienteering trails and a visitor's centre where they feed the squirrels so you will almost certainly get a good viewing. There are also peacocks on the island which are beautiful and dramatic to watch displaying to the females – it is less fun when you are camping and they call at all hours of day and night keeping you awake!

The island of Anglesey in North Wales also has a strong population of squirrels, around 400 up from a desperate low of just 40 in 1997 that are again separated – by the Menai Strait – from the competition of the greys. A Grey Squirrel cull and reintroduction of the reds to the adjoining mainland around Bangor hopes to see their recovery increase on the mainland.

On the mainland there are also pockets of Red Squirrels in the Lake District and Mid Wales. By far the strongest population of Red Squirrels is in Scotland – it is estimated there are around 120,000 in Scotland, 3,000 in Wales and 15,000 in England. The Queens estate at Balmoral supports Red Squirrels and they are still living in the highlands, south Scotland and the Grampians.

## HOW TO SPOT A RED SQUIRREL

Once you get yourself into an area to look for Red Squirrels it is not always easy to spot one.

Red Squirrels are much more elusive than their brash and fearless American cousins. They tend to hide away in the tree canopy and can be very hard to spot. The best things to look out for are their large nests or dreys up in the forks of tree trunks. Although usually quite solitary they will share dreys with family members in winter to keep each other warm. They do not hibernate in winter but store caches of food to keep themselves going, so even in winter you may spot them but they are likely to be less active. As well as the dreys look out for pinecones nibbled by squirrels. Nibbled pinecones look a bit like a corn on the cob with all the kernels chewed off; either end tends to be left unchewed giving it a slightly 'apple core' profile.

Red Squirrels are most active at sunrise and sunset particularly in spring and autumn and as you would imagine tend to have a rusty red coat. They are smaller than the Grey Squirrel with tufts on the ends of their ears, the tufts are longer and more distinctive in winter than in summer when they moult – if you are of the right generation think of Tufty from the Tufty Club or Beatrix Potter's Squirrel Nutkin.

As depicted by Roahl Dahl in *Charlie in the Chocolate Factory* squirrels can actually judge, by the weight of a hazelnut, whether it contains a juicy kernel or not and then don't waste their energy on breaking it open.

If you can't see the Red Squirrel you may hear it. It has a 'chuck chuck' call that sounds almost conversational. They also foot tap, like rabbits, when aggravated.

# Why does a dock leaf help soothe a nettle sting?

**Dock leaves and nettles are another of nature's little miracles. They both enjoy the same soils and typically grow together. Get stung by a nettle and you can just reach for a dock leaf, scrunch it up a bit, rub on the juices and the nettle sting will instantly feel better. Having very cynical children they used to think I was just making them do it as a sop until I explained the science behind it.**

The nettle has very fine brittle hairs on its stem very similar to a hypodermic needle. There is a swelling at the base that contains histamine and serotonin as well as small amounts of other chemicals. When you brush against the nettle the hair breaks and a sharp point penetrates the skin delivering the irritating sting.

Dock leaf sap contains an antihistamine that will help soothe the pain of the nettle sting. Don't rub too hard or you will make it worse, just dab it on or even better chew the dock leaf a bit and put on the saliva/dock sap mixture for the best sooth. Because there is quite a cocktail of chemicals in the nettle sting other remedies may be needed as well. Try some calamine to further ease the pain.

## THE BENEFITS OF NETTLES

Although nettles have a bad reputation as a result of their stings and their weed status they are actually great plants – we are cultivating quite a collection here at this very moment. There are many reasons that we should encourage nettles – not least because they are so easy to grow.

**Butterflies:** many of our most colourful butterflies rely on nettles in their larval stage, the caterpillars of the Red Admiral, Small Tortoiseshell, Peacock and Comma all feed on nettles.

**Ladybirds:** beloved of gardeners the young spring growth of the nettle is an important hunting ground of the voracious ladybird larvae which feed on the swarms of overwintering aphids attracted to the spring growth.

**Improve your compost:** nettles contain a lot of nitrogen and work well as a compost activator.

**As companion plants:** nettles contain natural anti-fungal properties that protect neighbouring plants, if you have precious plants susceptible to fungal attack put them in a clump of nettles.

**Fabric dye:** the roots of nettles produce a yellow dye while the leaves produce a yellowy-green.

**Food:** nettle leaves can be washed and boiled to give a spinach-like vegetable. The leaves are also infused to make tea that is reputed to be very beneficial to health.

**Textiles:** nettles are very fibrous and can be spun and woven in to cloth. During the Second World War the German army reputedly had uniforms made from nettle fibre as there was a shortage of cotton. Due to the environmentally unfriendly and unethical nature of much cotton production, nettle cloth is making a comeback.

**Medicine:** the nettle has been reputed to help many medical conditions but is particularly known as a diuretic when taken as a tea or juice. It may also help arthritis used as a tea, poultice and by stinging the affected joints which, though painful at first, then relieves the pain in the joints.

**The etiquette for naming species is very clear. It is deemed unacceptable to name a species after yourself, so scientists sometimes look to interesting sources when naming new finds. The vast majority of species were named during the Victorian era when taxonomy really took off but the species list is continually being added to as scientists explore and catalogue further in remote and inaccessible habitats throughout the world. You'll find some corking species names when you start to investigate.**

When a new species is described it is given a genus name (like a surname) a species name (like a first name) and an author. Unless you have found a new genus the genus is predetermined by an existing genus into which the new species fits taxonomically; the author is the name of the person who made and describes the new find – so that is where you own name can come in. The species name is the one where you can have some fun. Names in Victorian times were usually Latin or Greek based and often reflected some aspect of the new species, the way it looked or its feeding habits that differentiated it from its relations. Some were allocated to honour another scientist in the field or to incorporate some kind of theme – mythology is a common theme in the naming of butterflies for example: *Thecla betulae* (Brown Hairstreak), *Celestrina argiolus* (Brown Argus), *Polyommatus icarus* (Common Blue) and *Plebius argus* (Silver-studded Blue).

More recent naming has been a bit more off-the-wall. In some areas of research many new species are being identified and scientists are having to find many new names. Some scientists appear to have fixated on musicians' names: the wasp – *Mozartella beethoveni*, the moth *Fernandocrambus chopinellus* and a particular favourite of mine the mite *Funkotriplogynium iagobadius* – Iago is the Celtic form of James (or Jacob) and badius chestnut brown so this is a subtle tribute to James Brown.

There seems to have been a trilobite specialist who enjoyed his musical references in species naming. A genus of trilobites, the *Mackenziuruses* were named after the Ramones – *M. joeyi, M. deedeei,* and *M. ceejayi.* Another genus, the *Arcticalymene* were named after the Sex Pistols *A. viciousi, A. rotteni, A. jonesi, A. cooki* and *A. matlocki.* There is also the trilobite *Aegrotocatellus jaggeri.*

Terry Erwin at the Smithsonian has had much fun recently with his beetle species, calling the genus Agra variously: *Agra vate, Agra cadabra, Agra memnon, Agra vation,* and *Agra phobia.*

New species names must undergo peer review in a reputed journal but luckily reviewers also seem to have a sense of humour and many crazy names have survived including my personal favourite, the mushroom named as *Spongiforma squarepantsii.*

# Which flowers do bees like?

**Bees are one of the most important and busy insects in the countryside as they pollinate so many plants. It has been estimated that they pollinate around 90 per cent of all wild plants, which would fail to thrive and ultimately die out without them.**

Some flowers are more attractive to bees than others and there are a number of factors that will influence the bee's choice such as colour, flower shape and position of the plant.

Bees are unable to see the colour red, which just appears as black to them. Blue, white, yellow and purple flowers are the ones that attract the bees. You will notice when you are out and about that it is particularly the purple flowers that are buzzing and humming with bee life. Self Heal, Woundwort, Purple Loosestrife, Thyme and Marjoram, Lavender and Catmint are all very popular plants for bees.

The shape of the flower can also be important for the bees. Ornamental double flowers are just too much effort for bees that struggle to get past all the petals and so tend to be less popular. Tubular flowers like Foxgloves (right) are very popular with long tongued bees – such as the garden bumble bees rather than honey bees.

As with houses it is all location, location, location with flowering plants. Bees love the sun so the same plant in a sunny location will always attract more bees that a shady one. Additionally wind can be a real problem. Bees like sheltered conditions so a purple flower, in the full sun behind a sheltering bush or wall is pure heaven for a foraging bee.

In addition to the flowers, bees need a supply of water, you will often see them drinking in spilled water after watering in the garden. A supply of shallow standing water will draw in the bees.

## FLOWERS THAT BEES LOVE

What is also important to bees is that there is a supply of attractive flowers over a long season. Plants coming in to flower throughout spring, summer and autumn provides the best foraging conditions. Typical flowers include:

### Spring

Bluebell, Crab Apple, Daffodil, Cherry, Forget-me-not, Hawthorn, Rhododendron.

### Early summer

Foxglove, Teasel, Wild Thyme, Wild Marjoram, Self Heal, Clover

### Late summer

Buddleia, Cornflower, Thistles, Heather, Ivy, Lavender.

Beekeepers will attempt to locate their beehives to obtain the tastiest honey. Bees will take the pollen and nectar from a huge range of flowers to make their honey and each flower will result in a different coloured and flavoured honey. The best honey plants are those that produce a lot of nectar, grow in sufficient quantities to influence the flavour, attract the bees and make a tasty honey. Our local beekeepers tell me that Oilseed Rape flowers produce a very bitter honey while rhododendrons and azaleas will actually result in a poisonous honey.

It takes a lot of work to make honey. Each drop of honey has taken about 80 drops of nectar to

produce. It has been calculated that a standard 450g jar of honey equates to around two million flower visits. Given the vast quantity of nectar required to produce honey, a few samples of nectar from rhododendron will not cause a problem, beekeepers will know if they have a sufficient quantity of a problem plant in their area and will not use that honey for sale. But certain toxic plants such as Hemlock, Henbane and Foxglove produce good, non-toxic honey.

One very useful side effect of eating honey that contains nectar from a particular flower is that it prevents the eater from reacting to the pollen from that flower. Hay fever sufferers are therefore encouraged to eat local honey produced from the season that causes them the greatest problem. Local beekeepers have become attuned to this and will often now write the season that each pot was collected in as well as their bees foraging area so that hay fever sufferers can chose accordingly.

Gardeners have always known how important bees are and they were once referred to as 'little messengers of God' which was a way of acknowledging how important they were to our survival and affording the respect and protection that they require. Bees were always treated with respect by the beekeeper who would keep their hives informed of the latest news. Particularly important was to keep them informed of deaths in the family. If they were not informed there was a risk of the bees swarming or another death in the family. Some beekeepers would even dress their hives with black crepe to show they were in mourning. A birth in the family and family weddings were also important news and the hive would always be given a piece of cake whenever there was a family celebration. (Struthers 2009)

Bell heather          Hawthorn blossom          Thistle

Morris dancing is a fascinating and mysterious sport, undertaken largely by men of middle-age or older, wearing white clothes, ribbons and bells, in pubs across the country and accompanied by the drinking of quantities of warm ale.

There is a certain amount of jargon involved in Morris dancing which you need to know if you want to appear knowledgeable. Individual Morris dance groups are known as sides. The number of dancers in a particular dance is known as a set or sometimes also a side.

Further terminology applies to the standard roles that individuals take in a side (see box).

The clothing is an important element of the dance. Different groups wear different outfits that give their group their individual identity. The men often wear ribbons and bells tied around their thighs, calves and ankles as well as their upper arms. The women typically wear blouses and long

## Morris dancing terms

The **squire** is either the leader or the administrator of the side and often calls (announces) the sets in a performance.

The **foreman** teaches and trains the dancers and sometimes does the calling of sets in public in place of the squire.

The **bagman** keeps the 'bag' – the funds and equipment of the side, they will often also take bookings for the side.

The **ragman** is the costumier of the side, organising and often making the costumes.

The **fool** provides the humour in the set. He is extravagantly dressed and communicates with the audience, sometimes in mime.

The **beast** is also present in some sides and is dressed to look like a real or mythical animal. The beast, like the fool, plays alongside the main dancers interacting with the audience.

skirts, with ribbon adornments.

Although it has a long history in the UK, the beginning of Morris dancing is something of a mystery. Earliest records of Morris dancing come from Henry VII court in the late 1400s. Several theories exist as to its origins, the most popular suggest it evolved from 'moorish' dancing and entered the English from the Flemish mooriske danse. In the 15th century moorish dancing is recorded in Germany, Italy, Croatia, Italy and Spain and seems to have been a European 'exotic' dancing fashion. The exact route of its accumulation into English tradition is rather vague.

## Regional variations...

**Border** style comes from the Welsh-English border – Shropshire, Worcestershire and Herefordshire. They typically black their faces for anonymity and wear 'rags', clothes completely covered in ribbons and strips of rag that move and dance with them in the loose and lively style of their dances.

The **Cotswold** dance is based around Gloucestershire, Oxfordshire and Northamptonshire. The dancers carry handkerchiefs and wave sticks but otherwise wear quite simple trousers and shirt outfits often with a red tape crossed over their bellies. They often have a musician and a 'fool' or animal character in their dances. Dances are usually for six or nine dancers although solos and duos are also danced.

**Longsword** comes from Yorkshire. Each dancer has a wooden or metal 'sword'. Throughout the dance the men hold to their own and their neighbours sword in a circle. The Longsword is a rapper dance and involves swords known as rapper swords. It originates in Northumberland and Durham with five dancers and short flexible sprung steel swords. The groups sometimes also have a fool character.

**Molly dancing** is typical of the east Midlands and East Anglia. The dancers were traditionally all male with blackened faces. One would dress as a female – the Molly. The dances were feast dances that were danced to raise money during harsh winters

**North west Morris** as the name suggests has its home in the northwest – Cheshire and Lancashire, coming from the mills in the early 19th and 20th century. The style is quite military and involves a processional dance of nine men and women wearing clogs with metal taps with which to drive out the rhythm.

Henry VII was a big fan of Morris dancing and the dancers often played to his court, records suggest it was an integral part of important social gatherings in the late 15th century throughout England. By the end of the 16th century, the era of Shakespeare's, records show that Morris dancers were dancing up and down the land, not only in royal courts. Morris dancing is often mentioned along with Mumming plays and had developed a folk dancing element, being performed in all parishes at festivals by the mid 17th century. Before the 17th century very little is known about folk dancing in rural England – everyday life was probably not chronicled by the peasants in those days.

Morris dancing declined after the industrial revolution with only a handful of village sides continuing. The dances and regional styles have now been revived and were recorded in the 20th century from the surviving village sides. There was a rapid increase in popularity of Morris dancing in the 1960s with many new sides forming. There was much debate at the time over the inclusion of women in the sides, even though 16th century records show their involvement in early groups, there are now accepted men's, women's and mixed sides.

Morris dancing varies from region to region and the different styles are now named for the region in which they originated.

**Consider the local roads and main roads as you drive around the country or peruse an Ordinance Survey map.**

Roads develop where there is a need for movement. Right back in ancient times goods were being transported around the country. In the Neolithic era, flint tools were made in East Anglia and traded in the Lake District. Battles raged across the country requiring the mass transport of men. Vast structures from henges, cathedrals and castles were built, all requiring transport of heavy stones over many miles. Animals also make paths, with or without the influence of man, on their way to drinking and wallowing points and the best grazing or feeding grounds.

Roads survive though continuous use. So those highways that continue to be useful are kept clear by the passage of animals and people. Routes that are less useful quickly fall into disrepair and are overtaken by vegetation.

The vast majority of roads in Britain derive from ancient drove roads, rights of way and trackways that have been in existence for years.

These ancient routes will have ended up with their unique sets of twists and bends for all sorts of reasons.

## LOCAL ROADS

**LOCAL GEOLOGY** Old local routes, usually foot and bridleways would, as far as possible, have followed the contours to save tired legs and beasts of burden. Dips and hollows were avoided as they would be prone to flooding and bogginess. Large trees and boulders were skirted as were ponds. You can see in wild areas from the footpaths criss-crossing mountains and moors how these routes would develop. When two tracks get close to each other people anticipate the junction of the path and short cuts develop cutting across to meet another path. Even quite temporary hazards and blockages like a fallen tree will cause people to detour; once the blockage is gone the path continues on its circuitous route and so the path develops.

**LAND OWNERSHIP** Many of our local roads criss-crossing the countryside come from prehistoric field systems linking fields to settlements. Paths would develop around individual's properties as the land was parcelled and divided up between landowners. Many local roads are just a function of the boundary of one man's land with another. Even new roads and footpaths can be dictated by the boundary of land ownership as negotiations are made for rights of way.

**SQUATTERS**  Medieval unsealed roads were often very wide, multi-track routes allowing vehicles to detour around deep mud. Roads were often very fertile as the animals passing along would keep it well fertilised. As pressure on farming grew landowners would often encroach onto the highway and set up smallholdings on the fertile route. If allowed to remain, these squatters' properties would lead to bends and curves in the road. On ancient roads that are now sealed it is still possible to come across a rapid narrowing of

the road, this could be where a 'squatter' has seized a bit of highway and built a house with long narrow roadside garden. Once the road surfaces started to be maintained this narrowing of the route was set in stone.

**RIVER CROSSINGS**  River crossings are an important controlling factor on any right of way. Rivers are usually only fordable in a few locations and bridges are hard to build and expensive to maintain, so roads must deviate to get to river crossings. Bridges being so important and expensive were funded by settlements some way from the crossings, as they would all rely on their maintenance.

## LONG DISTANCE ROADS

Short journeys and local roads tend to link settlements but on longer journeys different needs take over. On longer journeys small settlements do not need to be visited, so major routes used to miss out the smaller settlements to keep the journey going. The early long distance routes were largely 'drove' roads for the transportation of animals to markets, often many days travel away. Drove roads often have quite long straight sections, however, these straight open roads were very exposed.

So periodically the drove roads would have an almost 90° angle inserted into in it which was intended to protect the drovers and their flocks and herds. These sharp bends are a particular feature of ancient drove roads. On a long drove, days long, food and watering stops were required. These longer drove roads would therefore need to detour and stop off at a settlement for refreshment and rest.

## ROADS WITHOUT BENDS

The Roman tradition of straight roads, with very few bends came about because these roads were built by military engineers. To a certain extent they were building them over trackless and houseless wildernesses so had no land ownership issues to take into account. Additionally, because they were the military and state funded they didn't need to take account of boundaries and land ownership – they had instructions to link two Roman settlements and that is what they did, in the most direct way. Roman roads were built in straight sections between sighting points; at each high point they would adjust the route making a straight line to the next sighting point where the direction adjusted slightly again – a large scale dot to dot. Some Roman roads, such as Fosse Way, had very frequent zigs and zags; it is believed they were built in the frenzy of war with less time to sort out the surveying in hostile territory, resulting in an atypically haphazard route.

What's so great about cowpats?

**The dung of sheep and especially cattle is a rich source of nutrients and provides the perfect breeding ground for a wide variety of flora and fauna. The world of the cowpat is rich and diverse. Before the dung even hits the ground insects and plants are already starting their lives in the world of the cowpat.**

As many as 350 invertebrates are associated with dung, some of which live exclusively on cow dung or require it for one stage or other of their life cycle. Species particularly associated with cowpats include dung and dor beetles, flies, coprophagous beetles and annelid worms. They are also abundant in bacteria, fungi and seeds. Birds love the cow dung for the insects and seeds

and can be seen tearing cowpats apart to get at their contents. Small mammals – voles and mice – also have a go looking for nutritious nibbles.

These animals feed on the dung breaking it down and recycling the nutrients back into the soil. In turn they provide a great food source for predatory animals. In areas where cows are not native these invertebrates are also not present and cowpats do not get reincorporated into the soil and attract infestations of flies and parasites. In some areas, such as Australia where this has occurred they have introduced dung beetles to try to ease the problem.

Dung beetles employ one of three techniques in getting the most out of the dung. They either lay their eggs directly into tunnels they cut into the cowpat. They may lay the eggs in the ground under the cowpat so the larvae are protected by the pat and then fed by the dung as their parents cut chunks off for them. Alternatively the adults make tunnels away from the cowpat and collect balls of dung that they roll over to their

excavations and then push into the tunnel for their larvae's delight. It is largely the larvae that feed on the dung. By aerating the cowpat with all their tunnelling around, the beetles are also reducing the release of anaerobically produced methane into the atmosphere and so mitigating the greenhouse gas emissions of cows.

In addition to the number of species living directly on the dung, each cowpat will have a rich mane of grass around it. Rain falling on the pat dissolves nutrients and creates a nutrient rich run off which fertilises the surrounding soil. Nutrients from the dung fertilise the soil feeding the grass and cows are deterred from grazing around their own cowpats so the mane of grass grows rich and strong. This microhabitat provides the perfect niche for spiders and bugs.

While many people are repulsed by the presence of cowpats they should be seen as a good thing. Don't forget the sacred Egyptian scarab was a dung beetle – the symbol of rebirth. Ecologically speaking, we love cowpats!

## Safety

The British countryside is about as safe as anywhere in the world. The number of dangerous plants and animals is very limited and most are nothing more than a minor irritation.

If you follow a simple code of conduct you should be able to steer clear of major problems:

### Be Responsible, Respect others and Respect the Countryside

- Park considerately if you take a car.
- Slow down for walkers if you are cycling.
- Follow the instructions of people working in the countryside.
- Leave gates as you find them and stick to paths unless you are in Open Access Land.
- Use gates and stiles – don't climb over walls and fences.
- Take all your litter and waste with you.
- Be careful not to light fires.
- If you have a dog keep it under effective control.
- Make sure you know where it is and what it is up to – that goes for the kids too!
- Keep dogs on the lead around livestock and in ground breeding bird areas.
- Check weather forecasts (and tide tables if appropriate) before you set out.
- You may be heading out into an area without mobile phone reception – let someone know where you are going and when you plan to return

Certain areas of the UK have a high risk of picking up ticks and the related risk of contracting Lyme Disease. Be aware of the risk in your area but consider checking for ticks where ever you have been out and about. Particularly high risk areas include: New Forest, Exmoor, Thetford Forest, South Downs, North York Moors, Lake District and Scottish Highlands and Islands.

### TICKS AND LYME DISEASE

Ticks are blood-sucking insects closely related to spiders. There are many species living throughout the UK and each one has a preference for feeding on different animals. Several of them will feed on humans if the opportunity arises. The one you are most likely to come across in this country is the sheep tick (which feeds on many different animals not just sheep).

Ticks can pass on diseases between animals and a particular concern is Lyme Disease.

Lyme disease is caused by the Borrelia burgdorferi bacteria. The early symptom of Lyme Disease is a distinctive bulls eye, circular rash that develops in the vicinity of the bite, flu like symptoms may also be present. There is no vaccine for the disease but it can be treated with antibiotics in the early stages of the disease. If untreated the chronic effects of Lyme Disease can be very debilitating rather like a chronic fatigue syndrome. There is a much greater risk of the disease on North America where the Deer tick is a particular problem.

To protect against picking up ticks in high risk areas wear long sleeved tops and long trousers tucked in to your socks, use insect repellents and stay out of long grass.

The longer a tick is attached the greater the risk of disease transmission but the disease can be passed on in less than a day. If you have been in long grass, in livestock grazing areas, then you

should check yourself and your children for ticks. Tick bites are not painful so you are not likely to be aware you have a tick. Ticks will stay attached and feed for up to seven days before dropping off again. Ticks will usually be attached around the legs of adults and the waist of children however they like warm areas so check the whole body and pay special attention to the groin, armpit, skin folds, neck and scalp.

Ticks should be removed using tweezers, getting as close to the skin as possible. Get a firm grip and pull hard straight out (don't twist), you want to get the whole animal out if at all possible. There are also small plastic tick removers that can be bought at vets and chemists that are really efficient for tick removal.

## USEFUL LINKS

All websites start with www. followed by the address written below.

### Getting out

*wildlifestrusts.org.uk*
*nationaltrust.org.uk*
*ordnancesurvey.co.uk*
*bbc.co.uk/weather*
*bbc.co.uk/tides*

### The sky

*cloudappreciationsociety.org.uk*
*darkskydiscovery.org.uk*
*bbc.co.uk/science/space*

### Give it a go

*geocache.com*
*dartmoorletterboxing.org*
*britishorienteering.org.uk*
*ldwa.org.uk* – long distance walkers association
*Ramblers.org.uk* – Ramblers Association
*dswa.org.uk* – Dry Stone Walling Association
*hedgelaying.org.uk* – UK National Hedgelaying Association
*btcv.org.uk* – British Trust for Conservation Volunteers

### Wild world

*plantlife.org.uk*
*ukmoths.org.uk*
*ukbutterflies.co.uk*
*britishbutterflies.co.uk*
*rspb.org.uk*
*buglife.org.uk*
*UKfossils.co.uk*
*Stone-circles.org.uk*

### General interest

*naturalengland.org.uk*
*CCW.gov.uk* – Countryside Council for Wales
*snh.org.uk* – Scottish Natural Heritage
*Forestry.gov.uk* – Forestry Commission

# Bibliography

Baker J.A. (1970) *The Peregrine*. Penguin Books

Barnes S. (2007) *How to be Wild*. Short Books.

Blyton E. (2008) *The Magic Faraway Tree* series. Egmont

Burningham J. (1999) *Cloudland*. Random House.

Countryside and Rights of Way Act 2000

Dahl R. (2001) *Charlie and the Chocolate Factory*. Puffin

Deakin R. (2008) *Wildwood: A Journey Through Trees*. Penguin Books

Evans B. (2005) *Scrambles in the Lake District – Volume 1: Southern Lakes*. Cicerone

Evans B. (2005) *Scrambles in the Lake District – Volume 2: Northern Lakes*. Cicerone

Field Studies Council guides – *British butterflies, day flying moths, grassland plants*

Fortey R. (2010) *The Hidden Landscape*. Bodley Head

Gooley T. (2010) *The Natural Navigator*. Virgin Books

Hooper M. (1975) *Hedges*. Collins

Jamie K. (2012) *Sightlines*. Sort of Books

Jenkins S. (1999) *England's Thousand Best Churches*. Penguin

Kieran D. and Hodgkinson T. (2008) *The Book of Idle Pleasures*. Ebury Press.

Kipling R. (1994) *Puck of Pook's Hill*. Wordworth Children's Classics.

MacFarlane R. (2008) *Mountains of the Mind*. Granta.

MacFarlane R. (2012) *The Old Ways*. Hamish Hamilton.

Magill M. (2010) *The Way To Bee – Meditation and the Art of Beekeeping*. Ivy Press

Mallory T. (1988 ) *Morte d'Arthur*. Folio Society

Manning M. and Granström B. (2011) *Nature Adventures*. Frances Lincoln.

Marven N. (1997 ) *Incredible Journeys*. BBC Books.

McDougall C. (2010) *Born to Run – The Hidden Tribe*. Profile Books.

Monbiot G. (2013) *Feral*. Allen Lane.

Milne A.A. (1971) *When We Were Very Young*. Dell.

Piersma, T. (1998) Phenotypic flexibility during migration: optimization of organ size contingent on the risks and rewards of fueling and flight. Journal of Avian Biology **29**, 511–520 .

Phillips Planisphere – *Latitude 51.5° North. Northern Europe, Northern USA and Canada*.

Pretor-Pinney G. (2006) *The Cloudspotter's Guide*. Hodder & Stoughton.

Rackham O. (1994) *The Illustrated History of the Countryside*. Weidenfeld and Nicholson, London.

Scottish Land Reform Act 2003

Shepherd N. (2008) *The Living Mountain*. Canongate.

Skinner B. (2009) *Moths of the British Isles*. Harley

Struthers J. (2009) *Red Sky at Night*. Ebury Press

Turnbull R. (2001) *The Book of the Bivvy*. Cicerone

Usborne (2006) *Usborne Spotter's Guide The Night Sky*. Usborne Books.

Wainright A. (2005) *Pictorial Guides to the Lakeland Fells*. Frances Lincoln

Waring P. (2009) *Field Guide to the Moths of Great Britain and Ireland*. British Wildlife Publishing.

White T.H. (1960) *The Goshawk*. Jonathan Cape.

White T.H. (1996) *The Once and Future King*. Voyager Publishing.

Yates C. (2012) *Nightwalk – A Journey to the Heart of Nature*. Harper Collins.

As I'm writing this, on the longest day of the year, the window is open and five metres away I can see a young Blackbird perched on a corner fencepost. Slightly ruffled, mouth still joker wide, preparing himself for first flight. He stands tall ruffles his feathers, has a preen, thinks about it, looks around … then settles on his haunches again. Content to wait a bit longer. I dedicated this book to my beautiful girls who like the young Blackbird are gearing up and developing the skills they need to eventually fly the nest. Life with them contains so much fun and activity and they are developing their own love of the outdoors alongside all their other interests. They have amazed me every day of their lives and I'm so proud of everything they are.

I would like to thank again all my family and friends who have helped me in so many ways in the writing of this book. For unfailing encouragement and support they have all been unbeatable. Lending me their children or taking mine off my hands as required, dog walks, runs, mini adventures and sometimes bigger ones.

Those requiring particular mention are:
● In my current envelope of country the Curtises, Hassans, Hebbing/Seerajs, Hudsons, Merrys, McDowalls, Perfitts; and from my first envelope of countryside Rosie, Alex, Ju and Ali and their families who we don't see nearly as much as we would like to.
● My brothers and sister, their spouses and kids – the Turner and Foulsham clans.
● My Mum who is to blame for so much of what I do and Dunc, with whom life is always an adventure – 20 years and counting!
● Those no longer with us who have all added to my sense of the countryside: my Grandparents – Madge and Bill Pratt and my father John Turner.
● Those dogs I love to curse who bring that little whiff of the country into our homes – Alfie and his mates Biff, Nutmeg, Soña, Oscar, Monty and new girl friends Lola and Fifa.
● Last but not least the real work on the book – thank you very much Lisa, Nicki and Bloomsbury for all the work you put in to the design, editing and marketing of the books.

The author and publishers are grateful to the following for permission to reproduce copyright material.

15 Shutterstock/Helen Hotson; 23 tr Shutterstock/Sergey Lavrentev; cr Shutterstock/Takamex; b Shutterstock/Rudy Umans; 24 l Shutterstock/Bocman1973; r Shutterstock/Adwo; 25 t Shutterstock/Adisa; c Shutterstock/Stefano Garau; b Shutterstock/C_Eng-Wong Photography; 27 tl Paul Sawer/FLPA; cl Paul Sawer/FLPA; bl Paul Sawer/FLPA; c Paul Sawer/FLPA; r Simon Litten/FLPA; b Simon Litten/FLPA; 28 Shutterstock/Andrew Astbury; 29 tc Shutterstock/Alexander Erdbeer; b Shutterstock/Wim Claes; 30 l Shutterstock/Inge Jansen; 31 l Shutterstock/Erni; 33 tl Shutterstock/Yu Lan; tr Shutterstock/George Dolgikh; b Shutterstock/Matt Gibson; 43 Shutterstock/Oleg Bakhirev; 49 l Shutterstock/Erni; r Shutterstock/Nigel Dowsett; b Shutterstock/Nigel Dowsett; 50 l Shutterstock/Mikhail Markovskiy; r Shuttesrtock/xpixel; 51 b Shutterstock/Vladimir Konjushenko; t Shutterstock/Katoosha; 68 l Getty Images/Geography Photos; r Shutterstock/NW10 Photography; 69 t Getty Images/UniversalImagesGroup; b Shutterstock/M. Unal Ozmen; 74 r Shutterstock/Tony Brindley; 75 r Shutterstock/Tom Gowanlock; 77 tr Shutterstock/Randimal; cl Shutterstock/Martin Fowler; cr Shutterstock/Damian Money; bl Shutterstock/Bildagentur Zoonar GmbH; br Shutterstock/chris2766; 79 tl Shutterstock/Mark Mirror; bl Shutterstock/Martin Fowler; 83 tl Nicola Liddiard; cl Nicola Liddiard; tr Nicola Liddiard; 84 b Nicola Liddiard; 113 Shutterstock/Maria Gaellman; 114 Shutterstock/Menno Schaefer; 115 Shutterstock/Erni; 116 t Tony Hamblin/FLPA; b Shutterstock/Andrew M. Allport; 117 Shutterstock/Chris Hill; Shutterstock/Phoo Chan; Shutterstock/L F Rabanedo; 118 Shutterstock/Archeophoto; 119 Paul Sawer/FLPA; 123 cr Shutterstock/Digital Media Pro; br Shutterstock/Schafar; 129 t Shutterstock/Viktor Kunz; b Shutterstock/Elliotte Rusty Harold; 132 t FLPA/Jan van der Greef/Minden Pictures; b Shutterstock/Menno Schaefer; 133 t Shutterstock/Bildagentur Zoonar GmbH; b Shutterstock/xpixel; 134 Shutterstock/Budimir Jevtic; 137 l Nigel Cattlin/FLPA; r Bob Gibbons/FLPA; 174 t Shutterstock/Rob Christiaans; 175 t Shutterstock/Flaxphotos; bl Nature Picture Library/Alan Williams; br Nature Picture Library/David Tipling; 190 Shutterstock/Photo Fun.